Do⌐

on file

CR⌣

Picts

and

Ancient Britons

Picts

and

Ancient Britons

An Exploration of Pictish Origins

Paul Dunbavin

A Third Millennium Publication

Typeset by Amolibros, Watchet, Somerset

Printed and bound by Professional Book Supplies,
Oxford, England

CONTENTS

Introduction

Few problems in British history have proved as intractable as that of the origin and ethnic associations of the Picts. For although we find numerous references to these early inhabitants of Scotland in Roman, Irish, Welsh and English sources, they have left us no historical texts of their own. So often we find the early Picts mentioned, almost as an aside, in histories of Roman Britain and the few references that we do have can be frustratingly vague. So who were these people: the tattooed barbarian enemies of Rome?

Perhaps a typical summary of modern opinion on the Picts would be that of the late Dr John Morris, in *Arthurian Period Sources* (1995). He was in left in no doubt that the historical Picts were Celts, confidently announcing, "The language of the Picts was a form of Gaulish, akin to British". When highly respected historians make such statements they can take on the aura of fact. Morris cites the earlier authority of Professor K H Jackson in Wainwright's 1955 volume, *The Problem of the Picts*, which has itself become something of a landmark in Pictish studies.

Yet it remains far from proven that the Picts were Celts. It must be admitted by all that the historical sources are few and contradictory. The reality is that if one seeks out those few references that supply some hard information about the early Picts then they amount to very little; and the archaeological evidence is equally mute. The Celtic hypothesis therefore rests more upon the eminence of the various scholars who have proposed it than upon the strength of the underlying evidence. As a student of myth and legend, it seems to me that the evidence of native tradition has been much neglected hitherto, in favour of the opinions of linguists and archaeologists. It is my dissatisfaction with so much that I have read which has moved me to undertake this investigation.

The present study will therefore focus upon the *origins* of the Picts, and of the various tribes who came together under that name; as such, it will not pursue the origins of their neighbours the Scots, nor the history of Roman Britain, nor of any other nation who may be mentioned in passing. Neither shall I dwell upon the details of the source manuscripts, which have been discussed by many able authorities. The nature of the evidence is such that numerous conflicting strands have to be unravelled. I have therefore drawn a boundary at the point where the Picts emerge into history in the mid-sixth century; this coincides with their conversion to Christianity, which effectively destroyed any cultural evidence of origins.

The reader should be warned that the present study will offer a view of the Picts that is certainly not the current text book standard. It will concentrate on the oldest traditions of Pictish origins, together with early historical sources, which suggest that the Picts were not Celts, as most scholars now believe, but "Scythians". It will put an alternative case that the Picts (or at least one of their dominant tribes) were Finno-Ugrian immigrants from the Baltic. It is my hope that this little investigation will give the traditions of Pictish origins a fair hearing and by offering a viewpoint that does not commence from a Celtic bias, thereby offer some new ideas on a tired subject.

The Traditions of Pictish Origins

The ecclesiastical historian Bede, writing in the eighth century, tells us that Britain was home to five distinct languages: Church Latin, English, Welsh, Gaelic and Pictish. By the twelfth century the Picts had been assimilated into the kingdom of Scotland and the Pictish language was probably extinct. Bede also relates a legend about the origin of the Picts. He says that they descended from a colony of seafarers from Scythia who took possession of Northern Britain, whereas the Britons had already claimed the southern part at some earlier time. It is quoted here in full, as it is central to the discussion that follows:

> When they (*the Britons*) had spread northwards and occupied the greater part of the island, it is said that some Picts from Scythia put to sea in a few longships and were driven by storms around the coasts of Britain, arriving at length on the north coast of Ireland...

> ...These Pictish seafarers, as I have said, asked for a grant of land so that they too could make a settlement. The Scots replied that there was not room for them both, but said: "We can give you good advice. We know that there is another island not far to the east, which we often see in the distance on clear days. If you choose to go there, you can make it fit to live in; should you meet resistance, we will come to your help". So the Picts crossed into Britain, and began to settle in the north of the island, since the Britons were in possession of the south. Having no women with them, these Picts

1

asked wives of the Scots, who consented on condition that when any dispute arose, they should choose a king from the female royal line rather than the male. This custom continues among the Picts to this day. As time went on, Britain received a third nation, that of the Scots, who migrated from Ireland under their chief Reuda and by a combination of force and treaty, obtained from the Picts the settlements that they still hold. From the name of this chieftain they are still known as Dealreudians, for in their tongue *dal* means a division.

Bede's version of the settlement of the Scots can be compared with many sources and is without doubt historical, but his statement that the Picts came from Scythia is usually discarded by historians. The point at which we may speak of the *Scots* as a nation in northern Britain dates from the settlement of the Dal Riata in Argyle from about AD 500 onwards, although earlier intrusions cannot be ruled out. Before that date we must regard them as a wholly Irish nation living on the Antrim coast. When the Roman annals speak of raids by the Scots on the north-west of Britain, it always implies raiders from Ireland; indeed the names Scotia and Hibernia are virtually interchangeable in the texts. After AD 500 Dalriada at first encompassed both Irish and British territory, but in earlier times we may suppose that the dominion of the Picts extended right across to the west coast. The ethnic associations of the west coast tribes however, are rather less certain.

The medieval *Scotichronicon* cites authorities that the Picts of Albion came from the coasts of the Baltic Sea; and extensively quotes from Bede's account. We are told that on their arrival in Ireland the Picts obtained wives from the Scots, who allowed them to settle peacefully; but they later sent them, together with many Scottish men-folk, to colonise the northernmost parts of Britain. Thereafter many more Scots continued to cross over and settle among the Picts, becoming an increasing source of fear and resentment to later generations.

Bede is the earliest reliable historian to offer an account of Pictish origins, but even he is citing traditions that were already hundreds of years old. Comparable traditions of a Pictish immigration are to be found in other early sources. In the *Historia Brittonum* (or "British History") attributed to Nennius there is an account that the Picts settled first in the Orkneys, whence they raided and occupied the northern half of Britain.

The Biblical synchronisms that he cites would imply a very loose date of around 300 BC for this settlement, but there is no indication of where the invaders came from. The later Annals of Clonmacnoise also tell us that the Picts came and married Irish widows, but their point of origin is not given. It is apparent from all these traditions that there were already some aborigines (the "Britons") living in Caledonia when the Picts arrived.

Although Bede gives "Scythia" as the point of origin of the Picts, he employs that name in its broadest sense; much as today we might use the term "Russian" to encompass many other ethnic minorities within that vast region. When early Greek and Roman geographers looked to northern Europe they saw only "Celts" and "Scythians". Pliny, writing in the late first century AD remarks that the name of the Scythians had spread in every direction, but was beginning to be superseded by other names. Indeed, Tacitus, writing a little later did not know whether to classify the tribes on the Baltic shores with the Germans or with the Sarmatians. The Scythians of Herodotus (c 450 BC) were nomadic horsemen, who ranged over most of southern Russia at that era, subjecting many other nations to tribute. Just as the entire nation of Germans were hidden from our view within early descriptions of the Celts, so the broad term "Scythian" might conceal any of a whole range of other eastern European nations, such as the Balts, Slavs or Finno-Ugrians.

From Irish sources the later Picts may be recognised under the names *Cruithni, Cruthin* or *Cruthneach* and it is generally accepted by linguists that this is the *q*-Celtic equivalent of a *p*-Celtic **Priteni* from which the Romanised name of *Britanni* was derived. The name survived as *Prydyn*, the earliest Welsh name for the Picts and occurs in the Taliesin poems of the late sixth century. Jackson's suggestion was that Cruithni was a name retained by the Irish for all the unconquered Britons north of the Roman province.[1] MacBain earlier suggested a meaning akin to Gaelic *cruth*: "form", "appearance" and related it to the custom of body painting and the tattooing that is described by a number of classical writers.[2]

The earliest application of the ethnic name *Cruithni* was of a tribe in Ireland and we find them mentioned in both sagas and annals. It is perplexing that we are never told that Irish Cruithni tattooed their bodies. M O Anderson points out that

1   Jackson, K H (1955), 158-60
2   Macbain, A (1892), 272

the name was not applied to the Picts of Britain until perhaps as late as the ninth century; rather that it had earlier been a name of the DálnAriada of Ulster and thus related to the Scots.[3] The situation was clarified somewhat by O'Rahilly: Irish writers referred to the *Picti* of northern Britain when they used Latin, or to *Cruithni* when they wrote in Irish.[4] However, the Cruithni of Ireland were themselves never referred to as Picts. Perhaps the safest conclusion is to view them as a tribe living in both Ireland and northern Britain, but while they may have formed part of the population of later Pictland, the reverse was never true. It is rather analogous to our modern extension of the term "British" to encompass both English and Scots, when historically it belongs only to the Welsh.

The later Pictish kingdom was also known by the name *Alba*, and the term *ri Alban* occurs as a title in the king lists. It is not certain whether the Picts themselves ever called their country Alba, except perhaps if they wrote in Latin. As a Scottish name for northern Britain, it appears to have derived from the name *Albion* applied to Britain by the earliest classical writers; and from the ninth century the Irish restricted its use to the Gaelic-speaking kingdom north of the Forth-Clyde line. Since the extant manuscripts date from after the unification of Picts and Scots, the name was then carried back into history.[5] The original meaning of Albion cannot now be traced with certainty, but it was naturally equated with Latin *albus,* "white" and appears to have led to much confusion for the learned Irish when they attempted to explain Pictish origins.

The extant historical records of Scotland date only from the tenth century onwards, although the manuscript copies themselves are more recent. They derive from Irish, Welsh and English documents and were all, to some extent, influenced by the earlier works of Bede and Nennius, and by the classical geographers. All but one of these texts were published by William Forbes Skene in 1867 and that exception is not of relevance to a study of Pictish origins.[6] Skene's work was monumental and has been of the greatest value to all subsequent historians.

It was Skene's intention to collate and publish all the extant manuscript sources relating to Scottish matters that predated the fourteenth century chronicle of John of Fordun, whose work was augmented by various other historians, such as Walter Bower in his *Scotichronicon* of 1440. These medieval volumes

3 Anderson, M O (1987), 12
4 O'Rahilly, T F (1946) 341-5
5 Ibid, 385-7
6 Skene, W F (1867)

were the first attempt to rebuild a formal history of Scotland, following the vandalism of Scottish historical records by Edward I of England. Fordun's chronicle is not at all reliable for the earliest period and shows us all too well how history can dissolve into myth upon the loss of records.

The traditions of Pictish origins can be seen to have mutated somewhat over time. The oldest tradition is found in a tenth century manuscript now held in the National Library of France.[7] It holds probably the earliest version of the Pictish king list and is prefixed by a summary of Pictish origins (known since Skene as the *"Pictish Chronicle"*) and contains a statement that it was taken from the Picts' own books. Thomas Innes in 1729 demonstrated that this older king list was in closer agreement with Bede's history than that of Fordun. However, Innes recognised much of the preface as merely a reworking of quotations from Isidore of Seville. It can all be seen as a compilation by some Scottish or Irish scholar, who had very little real history to hand other than a king list.

The major innovation in the Pictish Chronicle is that both Picts and Scots are derived as two branches of the same people. These are the Albani of Asia, a race of supposed white-haired Scythians, from whom the name Alban derived as the name of their country. The source may be traced to the Asian albinos described in the geographies of Pliny and Solinus.

The *British History* of Nennius was also translated into Irish and extracts from the manuscript variants were included by Skene. These sources introduce yet further confusion into Pictish origins, but we are again assured that the traditions came from the Picts' own books. In one version we find them linked with the Agathyrsi, a Scythian tribe mentioned by Herodotus and Virgil.[8] They are said to have first seized the Orkney Islands, and from there they took control of northern Britain, going on to establish seven provinces. We are informed that a body of them later emigrated to Gaul, where they founded the French city of Poitiers.

A more elaborate version links them with six brothers of the Agathyrsi from Thrace who again wander through Europe, before landing in Ireland, and from there they send out colonies to northern Britain. Yet a third version sees them as soldiers from Thrace who link-up with the Milesians before their settlement in Ireland. They became the Cruithni of Ulster and at some later time the Milesians exiled them to Britain. The

7 Anderson, M O (1949)
8 for example: Herodotus IV, 50; Virgil *Aeneid*, IV, 146

5

origins of the Picts are seen to become thoroughly entangled with the various legends of the ancient invasion and settlement of Ireland.

Once established in the north of Britain, the traditions converge. In essence, the story goes that the Cruthneach (Picts) descended from an eponymous hero Cruithne, who reigned a hundred years. Cruithne divided the land among his seven sons: Cait, Ce and Cirig (these three being described as "a warlike clan"); Fib, Fidhach, Fotla and Fortrenn. The story seems to be an attempt to represent the origin of the Pictish provinces; and these are further set out in a twelfth century document *De Situ Albanie*, which identifies them. Fib is clearly Fife with Kinross; Fotla is Atfodla — the old form of Atholl; Cirig is probably Angus and the Mearns; Cait is surely Caithness; and Fortrenn is Strathearn with Mentieth: the region west of Perth. The location of Ce and Fidach are less certain, but probably Ce is Mar with Buchan; and Fidach would be Moray with Ross.

The traditions of Pictish origins took on a further leap of evolution in the twelfth century, when Geoffrey of Monmouth published his *History of the Kings of Britain*. Whether or not Geoffrey drew upon real Welsh or Breton sources, it is clear that much of his material was invented; but he did not hesitate to incorporate real history and traditions whenever they were to hand. The mythology now evolves around *Brutus*, the p-Celtic equivalent of Cruithne and the eponymous of the Britons. He divided the island among his three sons Locrinus, Camber and Albanactus; the latter becoming the first king of Albany. These new ideas then found their way back to medieval Scotland where, in the prevailing historical vacuum, they supplanted the earlier traditions.

The Welsh translations of Geoffrey's history are collectively known as "Bruts", after Brutus. The revised tradition that they follow again echoes Bede's story that the Picts came from Scythia and sought wives of the Irish. Here however, their king is no longer named Cruithne, but Sodric, or Rodric, who came with his pirate ships and settled in Alban. There he was killed in battle by Marius, king of the Britons, and the survivors submitted to him. He allowed them Caithness to live in, but refused their request for wives; therefore they went to Ireland and obtained wives there instead. Hence they seem to have acquired the name *Gwyddl Ffichti* (Irish Picts). The Welsh triads similarly list these among three invading tribes who came to Britain.

It was these Welsh-derived sources that led Skene to believe that the Picts could not have spoken a recognisable form of the British language, but rather a kind of half-Irish dialect ancestral to Gaelic; a theory for which he suffered savage condemnation at the hands of the p-Celtic enthusiasts.[9]

Although the traditions of Pictish origin are seen to recur in a variety of forms, underlying them all is the oldest and simplest version found in Nennius and Bede. It says simply that the Picts originated from Scythia, that they were all male, and that they obtained wives from among the Irish.

9 Jackson, K H (1955), 131

History and the Sources

The earliest unequivocal reference to north British geography comes from Diodorus Siculus (first century BC) who gives Cape Orcas as the name of a northern promontory of Britain. The name simply implies the cape opposite the Orcades islands, visited by the Greek explorer Pytheas (c.325 BC). The Orkney Islands were frequently catalogued by classical geographers. Strangely, the Orkneys were listed among the earliest British provinces to submit to Rome following the Claudian invasion of AD 43 and some Roman writers seem to have regarded them as a part of the empire.

For our next glimpse of northern Britain we must await Tacitus, who describes the AD 80-84 campaign of Agricola. His geography is frustratingly vague and his ethnic detail a mere background to his father-in-law's achievements as governor of Britain. By AD 80, Agricola had pacified southern Britain and was ready to extend Roman arms to the farthest limits of his province. His was the first Roman fleet to circumnavigate Britain and to establish that it was an island. Despite the claims of later authors, it is evident that Rome knew virtually nothing about northern Britain before Agricola's campaign.

Tacitus refers to the northern natives either as "Caledonians", or simply as "Britons" and names only one other tribe. The Caledonians, he says, were thickset with sandy hair, a description that we may still recognise among many modern Scots; and he suggests that perhaps their origins were German. We hear nothing yet of the British custom of body painting, or the tattooing that is much emphasised by later authors; but a contemporary poet, Martial, does refer to "Caledonian Britons" and "painted Britons".

Agricola's third year saw him campaigning as far north as the Tay, into the regions that would later become Pictish territory. His fourth and fifth years were occupied in consolidating a line of forts in the central lowlands, before venturing still farther north. The sixth year saw determined resistance from the Caledonian tribes. After an initial victory Agricola appears to have pushed north along the coast, never straying far from the support of his fleet; the Caledonians retreating northwards before him. The Caledonii were not a unified nation. Tacitus clearly states that the northern tribes met to confirm their alliance with sacrificial rites and that one of their many chiefs, named *Calgacus*, emerged as leader.

Although we can determine by archaeology that the Flavians built camps as far north as the Spey, it is scarcely possible to determine where the various events described by Tacitus took place. The deciding battle was fought at a hill he names *Mons Graupius*, which can only be located as somewhere in the Grampians — perhaps the hill of Bennachie. Agricola reinforced his army with some local British allies, whom Tacitus says had proved their loyalty by many years of submission. The outcome of the battle was a rout of the Caledonians and the survivors then dispersed into hiding. The summer over, Agricola placed his army in winter quarters in the territory of the *Boresti* — a tribe whose location again cannot be determined — taking hostages to ensure their safety.

Agricola's successor established a fortified line along Strathmore and the Mearns, with forts guarding the entrances to the glens. The legionary fortress seems to have been at Inchtuthil on the Tay, guarding the main route north into the territory of the Caledonii; but within only a few years the Romans abandoned these northerly outposts and withdrew to a defensive line between the rivers Tyne and Solway.

There is no reason to conclude that Roman authority had entirely disappeared from the north. It was usual practice for Rome to establish tributary kingdoms on their borders. Such client kings had been permitted farther south: with first the Iceni and then later, the Brigantes; but no historical source attests to this north of the Forth. They may have left a protected client kingdom among the Votadini tribe. Their hill fort at Traprain Law, south of modern Edinburgh, was continuously occupied throughout the Roman period. Perhaps the same may be inferred of the Fife peninsula; for the Flavians built no forts there and it would clearly have been unsound to leave a hostile tribe behind the frontier forts.

A generation later, when the emperor Hadrian visited Britain (AD 122), he ordered the building of the great wall that now bears his name. In 142 his successor Antoninus Pius took the military frontier north again, establishing the Antonine Wall between the Forth and Clyde. They also constructed a new line of forts as far as the Tay, apparently to protect the Fife peninsula, but these seem to have been abandoned after 170 when the legions again withdrew to Hadrian's Wall. Most of these events have to be inferred from archaeology. The second century is something of a dark age in the history of Roman Britain. The written sources for the period, such as the *Historia Augusta*, are non-contemporary. They tell us little about the northern tribes other than that they were constantly troublesome throughout the century; a fact we may deduce in any case from the necessity for such formidable defences.

Our best written source from the second century is the Alexandrian geographer Claudius Ptolemy, who included a wealth of geographical and ethnic detail about Britain in his work on map-making; and this will be examined in greater detail below. Ptolemy drew upon the work of an earlier geographer, Marinus of Tyre; and it is quite likely that his list of tribal names reflects those faced by Agricola. He also names numerous rivers, capes, cities and tribes, among them the *Caledonii*; and in the core Pictish region of north-east Scotland he gives the tribes as *Venicones*, *Vacomagi* and *Taexali*. The Boresti of Tacitus are not listed.

By AD 197 we hear that the Roman governor Lupus was compelled to purchase peace from the northern tribes for a heavy price while the emperor was otherwise engaged in Gaul. In 208 they rebelled again, this time provoking the personal intervention of the emperor Septimus Severus. His campaign of AD 208-11 was described by a contemporary writer: Dio Cassius. He too mentions the Caledonii, but here for the first time, we hear that the other principal northern tribe were called the *Maeatae*; apparently these lived nearest the Antonine Wall, with the Caledonii beyond them. Both Dio and Herodian, writing of this campaign, describe the naked barbarians who opposed the legions. Herodian remarks that they tattooed their bodies with designs of animals; a practice similarly attributed to a section of the British population by Solinus (c AD 250). There seems little reason to doubt that this was how the Picts earned their name from the mouths of the Roman soldiers.

It is worthwhile to examine the disposition of the Roman forts after the Severan period. Now the camps are found not

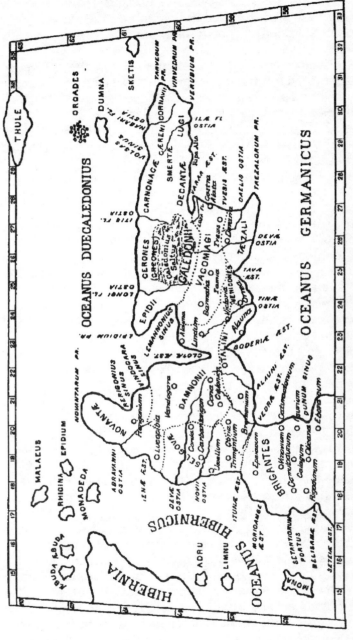

Figure One   The Map of Claudius Ptolemy (after McBain)

11

merely along the highland line, but also in Fife. A new legionary fortress was constructed at Carpow, where the river Earn flows into the Tay. Fife was now considered hostile territory. Carpow had a short life; Severus died in Britain and the fort seems to have been abandoned shortly after his successor Caracalla returned to Rome.

The Roman sources then remain silent on the subject of the north British frontier for the best part of a century. However from Irish annals we may detect evidence of a battle in which Irish forces defeated the Cruithni; and has probably to be dated at AD 237. There is no way to be certain, at this early date, whether the reference applies to the Caledonii, or Maeatae, or to the Cruithni of Ireland.

The Picts are first called by that name in panegyric orations to various Roman emperors. The Pictish era therefore opens at AD 297 with a brief reference in the panegyric of Constantius, which describes "semi-naked Picts and Hibernians"; and at AD 310 another orator mentions the defeat of "Caledonians and other Picts" by Constantius Chlorus, who seems to have campaigned against the Picts in AD 306. Although 297 is taken as the formal commencement of the Pictish era, these references seem little different from those of Martial two hundred years before. We may safely assume that "Pictish" language and culture date from a much earlier time; and that the name aggregates the various earlier tribes, one or all of whom must have spoken the Pictish language later described by Bede.

Our next window on the northern tribes opens with the Roman History of Ammianus Marcellinus. The fourth century was a turbulent period on the northern frontier. In AD 368 the Picts, in alliance with Scots and Saxons, again broke into the Roman province where they were defeated by Theodosius. Once again the tribal names have changed. Ammianus now divides the Picts into two tribes: *Dicalydones* and *Verturiones*, together with *Attacotti* who, although also a British tribe, apparently did not qualify as Picts.

These Attacotti are yet another new ethnic group, brought to our attention for the first time at this era. Shortly after the campaign of Theodosius, a corps of Attacotti (variants: *Atacotti, Atecotti, Atticoti*) were apparently recruited into the Roman army of Gaul. The barbarous habits of the Attacotti were also reported by St Jerome who, in one reference, seems to imply that they were cannibals. In another, he laments that his young Gaulish converts were not contracting proper marriages and were sharing their wives and children communally like the

Attacotti. He is quite specific that the Attacotti were a British tribe who did not live in Ireland; although they allied themselves with the Scots and Picts during the fourth century. They seem to have been suppressed by the other northern tribes, both before and after this period and are probably represented on Ptolemy's map under some other name.

A clue to the identity of the Attacotti is offered in the *Polyhistor*; a sixth century revision of the third century author Solinus. It holds a fascinating description of the Hebridean islanders and their customs. In Orkney and Thule no man possessed a wife. The king of the Hebrides, he says, was sworn to poverty and permitted no wife of his own, but he might borrow any woman he wished for a time, thereby leaving no identifiable offspring of his own.

Later historians and panegyric poets such as Claudian help us to fill in the history of the Roman Empire's decline, but they add little more to the our knowledge of northern ethnography. After the Roman abandonment of Britain we find the earliest native British references to the Picts in the scathing tones of St Patrick's letter to Coroticus; and in the somewhat pathetic report of Gildas (c AD 540), who describes the devastations wrought in southern Britain by the "foul hordes" of Picts and Scots. It is evident that in the post-Roman period the Picts were a major power in the land; in contrast to those divided tribes who had fled before Agricola only a few centuries earlier and who had to be "dug out of their hiding places".

Bede's description of the historical Picts distinguishes clearly between "northern" and "southern" Picts. The southern Picts, he says, were converted to Christianity by the British monk Ninian, probably during the early fifth century. The Pictish kingdom was at its maximum power and extent at that era. All that is known of the period comes from ambiguous references in the lives of the saints. The earliest is St Patrick (c.396-459) who speaks of the Picts lapsing into pagan apostasy; a state from which they were later rescued by St. Kentigern (c.518-603). The biographies of these saints are all much later compositions and must be regarded as less reliable in their references to the Picts.

By the sixth century, when Adamnan records the conversion of the "northern" Picts by St Columba, it is evident that the Pictish kingdom encompassed all of Scotland north of the Forth-Clyde line, apart from the recent settlement of Scots from Ireland, in Argyle and the Hebridean islands. Columba required an interpreter to help him perform his work among the Picts — indicative that their language was no dialect of Gaelic. Adamnan also records a battle fought by Aidan of Dalriada against a people called the *Miathi* or *Miati* who, as we shall see, were a southern division of the Picts. Columba encountered the Pictish king Brude mac Maelcon at his palace near Inverness and with the help of Bede we can date the commencement of his reign to about 556. Thereafter we move more certainly into history.

One other late reference must be included to complete the confusing ethnic diversity of the northern tribes. The southern Picts fell under the dominion of the Northumbrian Angles from the reign of Edwin (616-33) onwards and did not regain their freedom until the Battle of Nechtansmere in 685. It was during this period that St Cuthbert is said to have visited them. One biographer says he visited the Picts who were called *Niduari*; the other that he travelled to a region called *Niuduera*, which is clearly the same. This may be the name of a Pictish province, but is unlikely to have constituted a separate tribe or political entity at that era. It adds to the meagre list of Pictish words from which we may infer their ethnic and linguistic associations.

Later Pictish history must lie beyond the scope of a study of their origins. A little can be pieced together, mainly from English and Irish annals. The conversion to Christianity obscures the native customs and effectively destroys any cultural clues to origins. The historical Picts must thereafter be regarded as a part of the Celtic world, in the sense that they fell within the sphere of the Celtic Church; but it is surely unsafe to carry back such assumptions to the pagan era.

Shortly after their victory at Nechtansmere the Picts began to set up the symbol stones that are perhaps their best known artefacts. Thereafter we find their fortunes entwined ever more closely with the Scots of Dalriada. Around 710, King Nechtan, who was contemporary with Bede, seems to have ruled a strong and unified kingdom; but through a series of political intrigues the Scots laid claim to the Pictish throne. In 843 the Scottish king Kenneth mac Alpin ascended the throne by right of succession from his Pictish mother. Norse invaders ravaged Orkney and the northern coasts. Thereafter, the Picts and their unique culture fade from the pages of history.

The Pictish Language

Language and ethnicity are, of course, quite separate concepts. It is solely due to assumptions about their language that the Picts have been labelled as Celts. Bede's statement that the Picts retained a distinct language of their own, leaves little to suggest that it was anything other than a dialect of the Gaelic or British languages spoken by their neighbours; and most historians have been entirely content with this explanation.

Today, most European languages belong to the Indo-European family and this is evident at least as far back as Roman times. Prevailing theories concede that non-Indo-European languages were spoken in western Europe in Neolithic times. Celtic speakers are thought to have reached Britain only during the first millennium BC, displacing whatever languages were formerly spoken in the island.

In northern Europe the only rival to the Indo-European languages is the Finno-Ugrian group. This includes Finnish itself, Estonian, Lappish and the various Finnic languages spoken in Russia, together with the more distantly related Ugrian languages. These languages are thought to have developed immediately to the north of the Indo-European family, as they have borrowed extensively from the Baltic languages (see appendix B); and this is usually taken to imply a Finno-Ugrian homeland somewhere in northern Russia or Siberia. Therefore we should not rule out that any Pictish colonists, if they came from Baltic "Scythia", may also have been Finnic speakers.

Some of the earliest opinions about the nature of the Pictish language were based upon the mistaken belief that it was ancestral to Old Scots, and therefore a type of Germanic related to the extinct Gothic. John Jamieson in 1818 was prepared to concede that a dialect of Celtic may have been spoken among the Goths on the Baltic coast.[10] As late as 1874 his *Etymological Dictionary of the Scottish Language* still promoted the view that the Picts were Goths.[11] These views largely predate any study of the Irish sources and the analysis of the Pictish ogham inscriptions, both of which came to the fore only in the latter part of the nineteenth century.

Another nineteenth century commentator was Sir John Rhys, who considered the Picts to have been non-Indo-European, drawing his ideas from an examination of the oghams. Rhys rejected the possibility of a Finno-Ugrian language on the grounds that there was "no evidence".[12] He instead proposed that the Picts were related to the Basques, but hurriedly revised his arguments in the face of fierce opposition.[13] The Basque theory was quickly discredited and abandoned.

In a classic study, the German philologist Heinrich Zimmer upheld the view that Pictish matriarchy was the key attribute that showed them to be non-Indo-European (or "non-Aryan" as he put it); and that they should be considered as the pre-Celtic British aborigines described by Caesar.[14] He too dismissed the possibility of Finnic with the words: "The attempts to show that they were allied to the primitive Finnish-Esthonian population of North-East Europe scarcely deserve consideration". However he fails to cite the references he rejects. It may be that he was only reiterating the biased view of Rhys, whom he does cite — and soundly rejects. From an examination of more recent references in the *Pictish Bibliography* I cannot say that anyone has so far subjected the Finno-Ugrian case to thorough scrutiny. The studies by Macalister and Guiter, both based on the ogham inscriptions, have pursued the case for a non-Indo-European Pictish, but were both over-enthusiastic in their conclusions.[15,16]

William Skene's view was that Pictish was merely an early or parallel form of Gaelic, an idea subsequently revived to some extent by Fraser and Diack.[17,18] These ideas too, have been solidly refuted, one might even say ridiculed, by studies of

10 Jamieson, J (1818)
11 Jamieson, J (1874)
12 Rhys, J (1892)
13 Rhys, J (1898), 324-5
14 Zimmer, H (1898), 10-11

15 Macalister, R A S (1940)
16 Guiter, H (1968)
17 Skene, W F (1836)
18 Fraser, J (1923)

Gaelic philology.[19] There are simply too many words within the meagre Pictish vocabulary available to us, which could not be q-Celtic. Modern place names tell us that the Picts or their descendants in the kingdom of Alba must, of course, have converted to Gaelic speech at some point; but there is insufficient evidence with which to date this language shift.

The view that has come to prevail is therefore that the Picts were Celts and that they probably spoke a p-Celtic language, perhaps more closely related to continental Gaulish than to Welsh.[20] Thomas Innes favoured the affinity of Pictish to Welsh, suggesting that it was perhaps the original British language, untainted by contact with Latin; but it was further promoted by Stokes in 1890, who examined Irish annals and composed a glossary of every Pictish word that he could find.[21] The p-Celtic hypothesis was further developed by MacBain,[22] W J Watson[23] and O'Rahilly;[24] their opinions were in their turn summarised, leaving room for some doubt, by Jackson in *The Problem of the Picts* and there, to use his own words, "the matter rests".[25] He coined the name *Pritennic* to represent the p-Celtic element of Pictish. The Celticists have won the argument by sheer weight of numbers and few would now look beyond Jackson or Watson for an authority in this matter.

However, the subject of the Pictish language has not been left to rest and more recent contributors have further augmented the p-Celtic hypothesis. One recent interpretation of the late-Pictish ogham inscriptions has suggested many more apparently p-Celtic words;[26] and Smythe, in the first volume of *The New History of Scotland*, brushes aside all of Jackson's remaining doubts in a frenzy of Celtic enthusiasm.[27] Koch, for example, includes a discussion of *Pritennic* within a general survey of the Celtic languages.[28] However, he is prepared to include within its scope, many names that Jackson had not considered Celtic at all. So we have a kind of "creeping" Celticity: the Pictish language has become Celtic and thereby the Picts have become Celts, with no one ever having shown conclusive proof.

The various legends that proclaim a "Scythian" origin for the Picts have therefore carried little weight in this linguistic debate. Indeed F T Wainwright, editor of the 1955 volume, *The*

19	Diack F C (1944), 82	24	O'Rahilly (1946), 353-84
20	Jackson, K H (1955), 132	25	Jackson, K H (1955), 132
21	Stokes, W (1890)	26	Forsyth, K (1995)
22	MacBain, A (1892), 287-8	27	Smythe, A P (1984), 46-52
23	Watson, W J (1926)	28	Koch, J T (1983), 214-20

Problem of the Picts, was moved to completely dismiss Bede's report of a Scythian origin for the Picts, saying:

> At best it represents a tradition current among the Irish, and perhaps also among the Picts; but no concrete evidence has yet been produced to support the suggestion that the Picts came from Scythia, and the story must be dismissed as legend or literary invention.[29]

It is sadly commonplace for academics, particularly archaeologists, to dismiss legends in this way. Why should any modern scholar assume that they are better informed about the Picts than historians who were contemporary with them; or even, it would seem, better informed than the Picts themselves? Wainwright refused to speculate on Pictish origins, defining the commencement of the Pictish era as AD 297, when a Roman orator first mentions the name. Before this arbitrary date we are obliged to term them "Proto-Picts".

29   Wainwright, F T (1955), 10

The Proto-Picts

We must now take a closer look at the various tribes that came together to comprise the later Pictish kingdom. The earliest list of northern tribal names is that of Ptolemy and probably describes the ethnic divisions of the first century AD, before Roman influence disrupted the politics of the region. Many earlier researchers have examined the ethnic and linguistic content of Ptolemy's names. MacBain was convinced that Ptolemy's names alone were enough to prove that the Picts spoke a Gallo-Brythonic language, but most opinion since has been a little less enthusiastic.[30] Jackson was somewhat less certain about Celtic Picts than those who cite him. In his influential 1955 essay he finds only forty-two per cent of the names on Ptolemy's map to be "clearly or probably Celtic", most of these being in the south and west of Scotland.[31] However, of the core Pictish region of North-eastern Scotland, he says: "On the other hand, the four chief tribes, the Caledonii, Vacomagi, Taixali, and Venicones, have names which cannot be said to be Celtic with any confidence". Whitley Stokes before him was equally unable to suggest a Celtic derivation for these, and even the p-Celtic enthusiast MacBain failed to explain the Taexali.[32,33]

However, for many of the tribal names and geographical features on Ptolemy's map one may find meaningful derivations in the Finnic languages. The first and most obvious candidate for examination is the name Caledonia itself (Welsh: *Celyddon* or *Calidon*). In the account of Agricola's conquests (AD 83-4)

30 MacBain, A (1892), 267-8
31 Jackson, K H (1955), 135-6
32 Stokes, W (1890), 397-416
33 MacBain, A (1892), 287

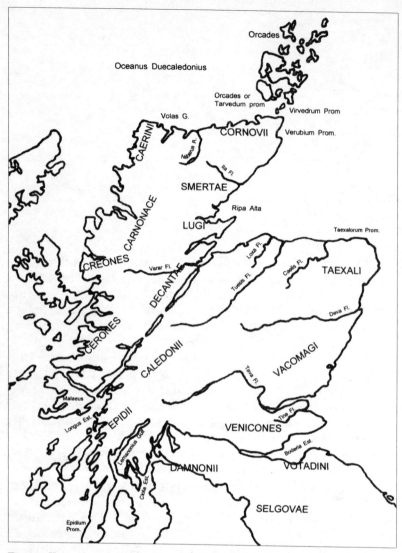

Figure Two A reconstruction of Ptolemy's tribes and river names on the modern map of Scotland

the term is used as if it were the name of the entire nation rather than of any single tribe. This is further confirmed by Ptolemy's use of the name: Oceanus Duecaledonius, for the northern sea. A likely Finnic derivation here would have to be based on *kala* "fish"; or rather *kalaton* — which implies "without fish" or "devoid of fish". This interpretation is of interest as it concurs fully with Dio Cassius, (third century) who tells us that the Caledonians entirely abstained from eating fish.

> Both tribes [*Caledonii and Maeatae*] inhabit wild and waterless mountains and desolate and swampy plains, and possess neither walls, cities nor tilled fields, but live on their flocks, wild game and certain fruits; for they do not touch the fish which are found in immense and inexhaustible quantities.

MacBain's suggestion that the name comes from a British *celli*, "woodlanders" would not explain why it also recurs in Ptolemy's name for the northern ocean: "Duecaledonius".[34] I can only suggest an alternative: "sustains no fish"; the Sea of No Fish; the Dead Sea.

Yet another of Ptolemy's tribal names that may have similar associations is Lugi or Logi, which is very similar to Finnish *lohi* "salmon"; and this region of Scotland is indeed noted for its fine salmon rivers. The fish symbol is also found on later Pictish symbol stones; and we may therefore postulate a community that revered the fish and considered it to be, in some way, a sacred or ancestral creature.

South of the Mounth according to Ptolemy's geography, lived the Vacomagi. The conventional view is that this name means something like "(people of) the empty fields", perhaps a miscopying of Latin *vacuum-ager*; for there are certainly other Latin names on Ptolemy's map, such as Ripa Alta ("high riverbank") and Alata Castra ("winged camp").

With reference to Finnish, we may attempt to decompose the name Vacomagi into two parts: *väki*, meaning "people" or "folk"; often used in a military sense to imply "men", "crew" or "forces". It has an alternative meaning: "strength" or "power". The second part of the name may be *miehet*, simply: "men", thus giving the whole name a meaning something like "men-folk" "strong-men" or "mighty-men".

Vacomagi may be entirely spurious as a tribal name. The topography of the eastern highlands makes it unlikely that a single tribe could have maintained a coherent territory across such bleak hills and indeed the name is never heard of again after Ptolemy. It could be a reference, misread from some local military map, to the disposition of the Roman forces dispersed along the edge of the highlands in their marching camps and forts. We should also note that Ptolemy locates four cities in

34   MacBain, A (1892), 287

21

the territory of the Vacomagi, which may well equate to the location of the Flavian forts. This would then overcome the contradiction that the Vacomagi supposedly possessed four cities, whereas Dio Cassius, writing a hundred years later, clearly states that the northern tribes possessed "neither walls nor cities".

By far the most interesting of Ptolemy's names is that of the Venicones, who occupied Fife and the coastal plain north of the Tay. Here, an equivalent in Finnish would be *vene* "boat" together with *kunta*; a word that originally meant "army", "crowd" or "group of people".[35] However when these two words are combined as *venekunta* the term implies "a boat's crew". This is a further remarkable coincidence, as it clearly supports the legend, related by Bede and others, that the Picts descended from an ancestral band of seafarers from Scythia. The variant form *Venecontes* is found in some Greek versions of Ptolemy.

This coincidence may be taken a stage further. That the Picts were a maritime nation is evident in Gildas' description of the Pictish raids of the early fifth century. If we examine the various Irish and Pictish additions to the Historia Brittonum then we find allusions to further migrations of Pictish people to Gaul; where, in Caesar's account, we again encounter maritime tribes named both Pictones and Veneti.[36] These tribes, we are told, carried on a regular commerce with Britain. Ptolemy's description of western Ireland reveals a tribe there named the *Vennicnii*. The presence of a tribe named the Venedi on the Baltic shores in Roman times, lends additional weight to the various migration legends. In modern Finnish, the name *Vene* can also mean "a Russian".

Another occurrence of this name has been proposed by Koch, who suggests that the name *Maes Gwyngwn* in the sixth century British poem *Y Gododdin* may be "Stone of the Wenicones".[37] The context of the poem does indeed suggest that this was a place in Pictland. This follows a conventional *p*-Celtic derivation that Venicones means something like "The Kindred Hounds" (**weni-*: "family", "kindred"; **kunes*: "hounds", "wolves"). The name *Gododdin*, of course, is the Welsh derivative of Ptolemy's *Votadini* tribe, whom he locates south of the Forth. They were without doubt Britons and their territory overlapped that of the Picts in the area around Clackmannan. Koch suggests that the "stone of the Wenicones"

35 Hakulinen, L (1961), 227-8
36 Julius Caesar, *The Gallic War*, II, 34; III, 7-11, 16-18; VII, 75
37 Koch, J T (1986)

may have been that at Clackmannan; or some other such stone in Fife or on the shores of the Tay, which served as a religious or political centre for the tribe. We must hold in mind that it is Ptolemy who gives us the oldest attested form of the name.

A city named *Orrea* is listed within the territory of the Venicones. The nearest modern Finnish equivalent of this would be *orja* "slave" (Estonian: *ori*), which if valid might imply that the Venicones traded in slaves. We know from St Patrick's letter to Coroticus that the later Picts (c AD 450) were quite willing to purchase slaves from the Britons.

On the assumption that the Venicones occupied Fife and Gowrie, it is also interesting that Ptolemy lists a river Tina, as lying between the estuaries of Tava (the Tay) and Boderia (the Forth) which can only imply the Fife Eden. Rivett & Smith conclude that this name must originally have been Ituna, after analogy with the Eden of Cumbria.[38] In this case one may suggest a Finnic *Itä* "east" or *Itäinen,* "eastern" or "easterly". The Eden is a comparatively minor river, so it may be significant that both it and the northern river Navar should be mapped, whereas more significant estuaries along the east coast of Scotland are omitted.

The tribal names of north-east Scotland offer yet more interesting possibilities. The Taexali occupied the area of modern Buchan and Aberdeenshire, as we may deduce from the fact that Ptolemy also lists a cape: Taezalorum Promontorium in this region. This name may have a Finnic equivalent in the verb *taistella,* "to fight a battle", or *taistelija* "a fighter"; there is also an older form of the word: *takistella* "to wrestle".[39] The name would therefore imply a fierce or warlike tribe. Once again, the tribe is not mentioned by later writers.

Dio's account of the campaigns of the Emperor Severus (AD 208-11) describes only the Caledonii and Maeatae, as having absorbed all the earlier tribes. The Maeatae, nearest the wall, were perhaps a confederation of Ptolemy's two southern tribes: the Venicones and Vacomagi — if indeed the latter were a tribe at all. Their name is still preserved in Myot Hill, and Fort Dumyat: a hill-fort near Stirling. The name Maeatae implies simply "the men", as in Finnish *miehet* and *miehittää* "to man", in the sense of "the ship is manned"; also as in *miehitys,* meaning "the manning" or "the occupation"; or in Estonian *mehitama*: "man". Indeed, the sense is similar to that of *väki*

38   Rivett, A L F and Smith, C (1979)
39   Hakulinen, L (1961), 258

above. All these names seem to imply a military subjugation and would again concur with the various legends of an all-male invading force.

The campaigns of Severus were an attempt to incorporate the whole of Caledonia into the Empire. According to Dio, the first campaign was indecisive and was concluded by an agreement that the Maeatae should abandon a large part of their territory — presumably the southern part in the vicinity of the Antonine Wall. When in 211 the Maeatae again revolted, Severus ordered his troops north with orders to slaughter every man, woman and child. The campaign seems to have resulted in a further unification of the north; for when next we hear of the northern tribes in 297, it is under the collective title of "Picts".

It is illuminating that Ammianus Marcellinus described the tribes who flooded across Hadrian's Wall in 368 as: "Picts, Scots and Attacotti". These latter he describes as "a warlike race of men, who with the Scots, were everywhere causing great devastation". We hear nothing now of the Taexali or Maeatae and are informed that the Picts comprised two tribes: Dicalydones and Verturiones. The former we may easily recognise as a variant of Ptolemy's Caledonii (possibly "the two Caledonias"), but the name Verturiones is more problematic. It has been suggested that this tribal name survived as Fortrenn (perhaps an Irish genitive of a conjectural "Fortriu") one of the seven ancestral provinces of the Picts; and the title "king of Fortrenn" occurs in the later regnal lists. There are good reasons to suggest that this name too may be Finnic, and may derive from the same root as: *voittaa*, meaning "to win a battle". In Estonian *voitja* means "victor", or "conqueror" and *voitleja* means "fighter"; *voidu* implies: "in competition". It may therefore be seen that Verturiones is merely another name like Taexali, with virtually identical meaning: a victorious, warlike, or barbarous tribe.

No obvious Finnic root can be offered for the name "Attacotti" which has surely been adequately explained as a British word, implying "very ancient ones" or "oldest inhabitants" — in other words "aborigines".[40] The Scots, as we know, were still based in Ireland at this early period, but the reference may already encompass some Scots among Ptolemy's west-coast tribes. The reference in Ammianus to Dicalydones must equate with the Caledonii, together with the half-Irish Maeatae/Venicones; while his "warlike" Attacotti may

40   Stokes, W (1890), 394

therefore be equated with Ptolemy's Taexali, whose very name, as we have seen above, implies these same warlike attributes.

Most of the tribal names on the western side of Ptolemy's map, offer few obvious Finnic associations; and it is here that Celticists have found greatest success (see appendix "E"). The Epidii and the lowland Damnonii, are generally accepted to have been tribes of Britons; Arguments may also be made for the Cornovii and Smertae as immigrants from the south; while such names as the Creones and Cerones resemble more closely the Irish: Cruithni. The northern part of Ptolemy's map is crammed with so many names that it seems unlikely they could all be independent communities in such a sparsely populated region.

There are also a few names from the earliest Roman sources that we may isolate as expressly Caledonian — as distinct from Pictish. These are the names: Calgacus, the chief who fought Agricola; and the battle that they fought at Graupius; Argentocoxus, a Caledonian chief named by Dio Cassius; and Uepogenus, a Caledonian remembered in an inscription from Colchester. There is nothing at all Finnic about these names and, Graupius apart, they can be convincingly explained as British.[41] But personal names are highly unreliable and could be translations; to say that Argentocoxus means "silver-leg" in British could be rather like concluding that Chief Sitting-Bull was English. The fact that Tacitus did not distinguish the Caledonians from other Britons is perhaps more indicative here. However, if there was indeed a p-Celtic element in the northern population then there are good reasons here to attribute it to the Caledonii rather than the Maeatae.

The Irish sources use the name Cruithni or Cruthin to refer to people living both in Britain and in Ireland, but when they employ the name Picti it always implies a people of northern Britain. The name was applied to some ethnic group much earlier than the first use of the name Pict by the Roman historians. It is worth stating that neither name is likely to have a Finnic origin. The later Norse invaders seem to have referred to the Picts by the name Peti, describing them as a race of dwarfs. Now if this were the original form of the name Pict then, were it to be Finnic, it would require an interpretation something like "deceiver" or "traitor". This seems a most unlikely accolade for a nation to adopt for itself and on balance a derivation from the Latin must remain favourite.

41   Jackson, K H (1955), 135

Place Names

Ptolemy's map of Caledonia names many identifiable geographical features, such as rivers and towns. It is to be expected that tribal and place names might preserve the language of the inhabitants at that era, whereas river names are more likely to be archaic and aboriginal. Some of Ptolemy's names offer further challenging possibilities. As we have seen, Lugi was perhaps not a tribal, but a regional name. Another possibility in this category might be Caerini, from Finnish *karinen*: "rocky", "reefy", describing the craggy western coastline.

The river Caelis, identifiable with the modern Deveron, may derive from a Finnic *kahla-us*, "ford", from *kahla* "wader"; and therefore implying a river that could be forded. Near it was the Tuesis estuary (probably the Spey): perhaps *tuhis* — the "hissing" river. The Loxa is apparently the river Lossie and *lossi* is a modern Finnish word meaning "ferry". Farther north is marked the Varar estuary: usually equated with the River Farrar that flows into the Beauly Firth. This name would imply the "crooked" estuary, from Finnish *väärä*, "bent, crooked, twisted"; and a glance at any map of Scotland will again reveal how appropriate this name is. Ptolemy's Nabarus is clearly the modern river Navar of Caithness; compare this name with the Neva of St Petersburg, which is a Karelian word meaning "a treeless peat bog".

There are some strong reasons then, to suggest that Ptolemy's geography of northern Britain was ultimately derived from a Finnic speaking source with local knowledge. It was set down partly in Latin, partly in a local language, by an interpreter who knew the Roman alphabet.

The modern map of north-east Scotland shows the spread of Gaelic place names into the former Pictish region since the Scots of Dalriada absorbed the Pictish Kingdom in the ninth century. The presence of q-Celtic names within the former Pictish region therefore proves little about the nature of the Pictish language or of its predecessors. The presence of p-Celtic names in the north-east, such as those in *aber-*, *lan-* and others, is less easily explained, but it is surely significant that none of these obviously p-Celtic names are found on our oldest source: Ptolemy's map. This must suggest that they were introduced by later immigrants from the south.

The earliest reference of all is the Cape Orcas mentioned by Diodorus, which may date from as early as the voyage of Pytheas (c 325 BC) and certainly dating to no later than the first century BC. This name is generally given as Irish for: "the young pigs" and Watson inferred from it a tribal name Orcoi: "Boars".[42] However, the same root also occurs in other Indo-European languages and is the same root as English "pork". It was also absorbed early into the Finno-Ugrian languages, for example Finnish *porsas* "piglet". The name is clearly of ancient origin recorded in a Greek form. It has survived Norse invasions and could equally predate any Pictish settlement. It is often stated that Orcas/Orcades proves the presence of Irish settlement in the north as early as 325 BC, but in truth, a single word can prove very little.

A later Pictish place-name in the vicinity of the Antonine Wall is offered by Bede. This is *Peanfahel*, the name that the Picts applied to the monastery at Kinneil near Abercorn. This is one of the few indisputably Pictish words that we possess; and the theories that Pictish was a Celtic tongue have placed great emphasis upon this single word.[43] One hypothesis is that it was part p-Celtic, part q-Celtic, based on the assumption that *pean* was a Pictish equivalent of Cumbric *pen,* or Gaelic *ceann*; and fahel would be Gaelic *fáil*, which would translate the entirety as "head of the wall" — implying that it lay near the western end of the Antonine Wall.[44]

The analogy with Finnish suggests an alternative. The name might equally be a compound based upon a Finnic root *pyhä* (Estonian: *püha*) meaning "holy" or "sacred"; as found in *pyhäin,* "sacrilage" and *pyhäkko,* "sanctuary" or "shrine". The nearest modern Finnish equivalent of Peanfahel would appear

42   Watson, W J (1926), 28-9   44   Nicolaisen, W F (1976), 171
43   Jackson, K H (1955), 143-4

to be *Pyhiinvaellus*, which means "pilgrimage" or literally "holy-wandering". This would concur well enough with the context that the name is used by Bede, as one might expect a monastery to become a place of pilgrimage. Was it not from here that Bishop Trumwine served as Bishop of the Picts during the brief Northumbrian occupation of southern Pictland?

This exploration may also be extended to many modern place names from the former Pictish region. The most widely occurring of these are the various place and river names beginning *al*, of which obvious examples would be Alness on the Cromarty Firth, Strathallan and Alloa; often considered to be pre-Celtic, this prefix has a very ancient pedigree in the Finno-Ugrian languages, being found even in Hungarian. It usually conveys the sense "low" or "down" as found in *alanko*, "lowlands"; *alas*, "down" or *alue*, "territory"; as is found, for example, in *Alankomaat* — the modern Finnish name for the Netherlands.

Other possibilities found on the modern map, are the names Mar and Braemar, which may derive from *maa*, meaning "the land", "earth", or "ground". A further similarity occurs in the names Ullapool and Unapool on the west coast of Sutherland. The former is usually given as Norse "Olaf's Bol" — the settlement of Olaf;[45] but it seems to have much in common with *Ullapala*, a name found in one of the Finnish Kalevala songs and meaning "place by the open water".[46]

An examination of the modern map of Scotland will suggest many other candidates for a Finnic derivation, but it is perhaps best to restrict the present analysis to names that are usually considered non-Celtic. Unfortunately, the place names of north east Scotland have undergone so many sound changes; most names on the modern map are corrupt Old-Scots renderings of Gaelic names, which may themselves disguise an original Pictish name. It is also unfortunate that in the area where we might have expected many Pictish names to survive: Orkney and Caithness, they have been almost entirely wiped out by later Norse names.

For most place names in Scotland a Norse, Gaelic or Cumbric root can usually be suggested, but this could be misleading. To give just one example, in Finnish, the word *kylä* is an ancient word meaning village or hamlet and this may underlie a few of the Kil- or Kyle place-names of Scotland: such as Kilconquhar, Kylestrome and so forth. Most such names are without question derived from Gaelic *cill*, "church", rather

45   Darton, M (1990), 275
46   Kirby, W F (1907) republished (1985), 665

than any postulated Finnic-Pictish *kylä*. Many other Finnic roots could be similarly masked by Celtic names of equivalent sound.

One class of names for which it is difficult to argue any Norse or Gaelic root, are the *Pit-* names, such as Pitmedden, Pitlochry and others. The second part of these names is usually Gaelic; and their distribution is entirely restricted to the territory of the "historical Picts".[47] An old form: *pett* has been suggested; in the twelfth century Book of Deer it seems to have been as much a unit of population as of land.[48] The Celticists have had to resort to Gaulish to find a *p*-Celtic root for this, citing Gaulish **petia* — a piece (of land) or an estate.[49] Following the Finnic hypothesis however, another possibility is that the Pit-names derive from the same Finnic root as *pitäjä*, meaning "parish", or perhaps originally "taxpayer-district".[49] This may explain the widespread retention of such a place-name element after the Scots assimilated the Pictish kingdom. Another possibility here is that the Pit-names represent converted Christian parishes, which would explain why comparatively few occur in northern Pictish territory where Christianity arrived late and was never strong.

Philologists will only usually admit a classification of pre-Celtic or non-Indo-European when they can find no Celtic root at all — however obscure. Nicolaisen, for example, cited the German Indo-Europeanist Hans Krahe, who believed in an "Old European" nomenclature underlying the river names of Europe.[51] If I may quote him here:

> "...Scotland and Britain share that Old European river-nomenclature and that, therefore, when the Celts first arrived in Scotland, there were already people present who, as immigrants from Europe centuries before them had introduced an Indo-European language to the British isles."

He, of course, took it as read that the Picts were Celts and is discussing here even earlier peoples. Whatever the merits of such analyses, they are entirely invalidated if the Picts were intrusive, non-Indo-European, "Scythians" as all the traditions indicate; and particularly so if their language already carried Indo-European loan words within it.

47	Watson, W J (1926), 407	50	Hakulinen, L (1961), 229 & 258
48	Jackson, K H (1972), 114-116	51	Nicolaisen, W F H (1976), 191
49	Jackson, K H (1955),148; Stokes (1890), 412		

Ethnic Origins

A further strong clue to Pictish ethnic origins is offered by Tacitus. In his account of Agricola's campaign in the north of AD 80-84, he refers to all the natives simply as Britons (*Britanni*) and makes no distinction between the Britons of the Roman province and those of Caledonia. It is clear that Tacitus knew British to be a Celtic language, for he tells us so elsewhere.[52] Neither should it be forgotten that he also quotes extensively the speech of Calgacus, which this chief of the Caledonii is said to have made to his troops before the battle of Mons Graupius. If genuine (as to which there must be serious doubt) then Tacitus must surely have translated the gist of the speech from a native British tongue.

This may be significant since, in his own *Germania*, Tacitus describes a tribe on the Baltic shores, called the *Aestii*. He admits being uncertain how to classify this tribe; as their customs were German, but their language was, he says, "more like that of the Britons". To some of course, this would imply the presence of Celts on the Baltic shores, but Tacitus includes the Aestii among the greater Suebian nation, along with the Goths and the Angles. This takes us back again to the root of nineteenth century notions that the Picts were Goths.

However, the Aestii are arguably the same nation that Pliny and Mela called Essedones: the Issedones of Herodotus. As the Aestii are usually identified with the ancestors of modern Finns and Estonians, the observation by Tacitus would therefore suggest that one of the languages spoken in first century Britain was related to modern Estonian and therefore an early Finnic

52   Tacitus, *Germania* 43 - see Sources

language. Since we can be confident that the southern British spoke Brythonic, the inescapable conclusion must be that this other language was spoken north of the Roman province.

Whitley Stokes suggested that the Boresti of Tacitus was Latin and simply implied "a northern tribe" from a poetic Latin *Boreas*.[53] The "B" sound is entirely foreign to Finnic languages. It is perhaps coincidence, but this may be our earliest historical reference to the Scythian invaders. Tacitus may have been referring to a people who came from the region of the river Boresthynes (the modern Dnieper of Belarus). It is known that Finnic nations lived around the northern reaches of this river during the earliest recorded times.

It is therefore interesting to see how far back the analogy with Finnic can be extended; Finnish is regarded as the most conservative of the Finnic languages and most of the roots suggested here go back at least to Common Finnic (c 1000 BC to AD 100). If some of the names on Ptolemy's map may indeed be regarded as Finnic, then the two languages must have diverged well before the Christian era. We may therefore view the Pictish migration as part of the general dispersal of the proto-Finns that, according to linguistic analysis, occurred shortly before the Christian era.

53   Stokes, W (1890), 395

The Pictish King Lists

We may be reasonably certain that no Pictish "invasion" of northern Britain occurred during Roman times, although it is just possible that the sparse historical record has failed to record it; the legends of Pictish origins are all found in much later documents, set down as much as a thousand years after the events. The king lists attached to the *Pictish Chronicle* and the Irish Nennius do offer a chronology, which if viewed uncritically, would predate the Roman invasions. These are the only documents that might have preserved the Picts' own knowledge of their history.

William Skene listed seven versions of these king lists; the oldest dating from the tenth century, the most recent from the fourteenth century. They have each been copied many times before arriving at their extant manuscripts. There are many inconsistencies in the regnal years and the names of the kings show a range of variant spellings between the lists, often being rendered in Irish forms. Some of the earliest entries are very strange indeed and it is hardly surprising that they should have been miscopied by the scribes. The majority of Skene's glossary of "Pictish words" were merely personal names derived from these lists.[54]

Despite the various discrepancies there is enough evidence to group the king lists into two families; each of which has derived from a long-lost master list. These two master lists were most likely maintained at different

54   Skene, W F (1876-80), 501-9
55   Cummins, W A (1995), 15-21

monastic centres, drawing upon similar oral traditions for their earliest entries.[55]

The kings are regarded as historical after Brude son of Maelchon (554-584) who received Saint Columba at his court, but they appear to go all the way back to the legendary eponymous Cruithne at around 500 BC. Although there is no independent confirmation, there is every possibility that the reigns immediately before Brude are equally valid. By counting back the reigns we find a king Drust, who "fought a hundred battles", and who may have been responsible for the southern raids much lamented by Gildas. The earlier names become increasingly exotic; and before we could apply etymology to such names as Canatulacma, Usconbest or Deocillimon, we would have to decide which of the written forms is the most faithful to the original Pictish pronunciation. It is not even safe to assume that the names are Pictish. In the historical period we see evidence of intermarriage with Scots, British and Northumbrian royal lines; similarly these earliest names could indicate that the father came from an aboriginal tribe.

Still further back we come to the era of the "thirty Brudes", apparently an inter-regnum when for a hundred and fifty years, thirty chiefs of this title shared power. We must regard the Brude list as a native Pictish tradition, for the chronicle says that it came "from the books of the Cruthneach". The name "Brude" we are told is both the name of all the kings and of their divisions. The *Scotichronicon*, claims that before Cruithne the Picts had been ruled not by kings but by "judges". It is possible that the thirty Brudes represent a period of democratic rule like that ascribed to the Caledonii and Maeatae by both Tacitus and Dio Cassius; for the chronicle says that "Alban was without a king for all that time". However, no reference to the Roman period is at all evident within any of the king lists.

The ingenious suggestion of J T Koch is that the Brude-list records an oral-chant that has been misrecorded with the title repeated: "*after Gest Brude, Pont Brude; after Pont Brude, Leo Brude ...*"[56] That the name "Brude" represents a Pictish title or rank seems undeniable. One alternative that I shall offer is that the Thirty Brudes may represent a list of Pictish heroes. The names are always paired, for example: Brude Gest, Brude Ur-gest, etc. This *Ur-* prefix may recall a Finnic *uros* "male"; there is also *urho* "hero" or "champion" and *urhea* "brave",

56   Koch, J T (1983), 219-20

"heroic". Thus the list would read: *"Brude Gest, Brave - Brude Gest; Brude Pont, Brave - Brude Pont"* and so on.

The king lists do seem to confirm that Pictish royal succession was always through the female line. Other than the anomalous Cruithne and his seven sons no Pictish king was ever succeeded on the throne by his own son. Bede and the Irish commentators devise numerous reasons why this custom prevailed, so that the kings of the Picts should always be descended from an Irish mother. However, we do not need any of the complex devices, ancient or modern, that have been proposed to explain the matrilineal succession. It arises naturally out of the communal crèche system of the aboriginal inhabitants, in which no formal marriages existed and therefore the father of the offspring could never be determined. The society could be none other than matrilineal, as there simply was no male line of inheritance.

There can be no doubt that the matrilineal succession was ancient and aboriginal. Caesar attributed wife-sharing to "aborigines" and it was also practised by the Attecotti, whose name means "aborigines". The same custom was also attributed to the Scots by St Jerome; to Hebridean and Orkney islanders by Polyhistor; and to the Caledonii and Maeatae by Dio Cassius. We may presume that monogamous marriage was introduced only by the Christian Church, which would certainly have condemned the old way of life.

There is little else in the king lists that might help us with Pictish origins, but they do perhaps serve to establish an era for the arrival of any "Scythian" invaders. Some of the more conjectural possibilities are explored a little further in Appendix D.

Oghams and Symbol Stones

The Pictish symbol stones and the curious inscriptions that are found inscribed upon a few of them are conventionally dated no earlier than the 7th and 8th centuries. Although, strictly speaking, such artefacts lie beyond the scope of a study of Pictish origins they may still offer some clues to this end. They were comprehensively classified by Joseph Anderson and Romilly Allen in 1903, in *The Early Christian Monuments of Scotland*, who divided the monuments into three classes.

The Class I stones hold incised symbols and are thought to date from the late pagan period. The Class II stones also display the symbols, but now carved in relief and usually accompanied by the sign of the cross or some other device of the Celtic Church. Their distribution is restricted to the boundaries of the later Pictish kingdom, from Lothian to the Isles. The presence of the Christian cross on the later stones, strongly suggests that their purpose was religious and therefore, by extrapolation, might suggest that the other symbols also conveyed some pagan religious significance.

The Pictish symbols may be classified into two groups: geometric designs and animals. Anthony Jackson has recently attempted a reclassification of these designs, suggesting that the symbols occur in pairs, indicating marriages between lineages within a system of matrilineal families; each symbol being the arms of a family. This interesting theory remains to be proven. Earlier suggestions for the purpose of the stones include: grave stones of kings (*Diack 1944*), commemorations of the dead (*Thomas 1963*), territorial markers (*Henderson 1971*) or simply a kind of decorative art (*Stevenson 1955*).

Figure Three   A selection of symbols from Pictish symbol stones. From top left to bottom right they are: the "Pictish beast" (an elephant?), fish (salmon), horse, boar or pig, bull and eagle.

Since so little is known about the origin and history of the Picts, many books about them have been padded-out with copious pages devoted to pictures of these stones and their symbols. As Elizabeth Sutherland points out in her recent book, *In Search of the Picts*: after we have studied the symbols, "How much more do we know about the Picts? Precious little". She draws our attention to the figure of a Pictish warrior carved on an ancient stone near Collessie in Fife.[57] This depicts a naked figure carrying a long rectangular shield and a spear with a round apple; fitting in every way the description of the warriors of the Maeatae as given by Herodian and Dio Cassius. However, there is one other detail not supplied by these writers: the warrior also has his hair tied on the top of his head after the fashion of the Suebian knot (see appendix A). Unfortunately the stone is so worn that it is not possible to make out any other symbols. A Class II stone from Inchbraoch (now in Montrose Museum) also depicts the grooming of long hair into

57   Sutherland, E (1994), 174-5

an elaborate pony-tail, but here with the end curled-up into a spiral, rather like that found in the mane of the "Pictish Beast".

Perhaps more important than the symbols is that many of the stones also hold inscriptions written in the Irish ogham alphabet; usually assumed to be a late introduction that came along with the Celtic Church. When transliterated, these appear to be in an unknown and indecipherable language. Not all the known inscriptions are on stones; some occur on portable artefacts. Any relationship between the oghams and the symbols must be mere conjecture.

Many theories about the Pictish language have been based upon attempts to interpret these strange inscriptions. It was the oghams that led Rhys to propose that Pictish was not only non-Celtic, but also non-Indo-European;[58] a theory that was re-examined by the Frenchman Guiter who similarly favoured Basque.[59] Others, such as Macalister, have thought they could identify recognisable Irish words and names amid the unintelligible mass. Anthony Jackson, in his study of the symbol stones, has argued that the inscriptions may not be a language at all, but rather a system of numbers and dates.[60] In general, those who have approached the Pictish language from the analysis of place names, or the king lists, have come to the conclusion that it was a type of Celtic; those who have looked at the ogham inscriptions generally conclude that it was non-Indo-European. K H Jackson's view was therefore a compromise, that perhaps the language of a group of pre-Celts had survived in the north, within a mainly Celtic-Pictish kingdom. We should not forget that Bede knew only a single Pictish language and he was closer to the events than any modern scholar.

To take as an example the inscription from Lunnasting, Shetland, which transliterates as:

etocuhetts ahehhttannn hccvvevv nehhtons

This is the longest of the inscriptions and the most often quoted, as it conveys the extent of the difficulties quite adequately. The doubling, even tripling of consonants renders it unpronounceable, and leads to a conclusion that perhaps the oghams were not used by the Picts to convey the same sounds as in Irish. The group *nehhtons* has been equated with the Pictish royal name Nechtan: the Naiton of Bede. Suggested recognisable groups from other inscriptions include: *maqq*

58   Rhys, J (1892)   60   Jackson, A (1984), 175-200
59   Guiter, H (1968)

(Gaelic: "son of"), *crroscc* (Gaelic: "cross"), *dattrr* (Norse: "daughter") and *eddarrn* (a Pictish personal name: Edern) and perhaps also found within the *Pidarnoin* inscription of the Fordoun slab.

So what, if anything, can these late monuments and their inscriptions tell us about the origins of the Picts? It is dangerous to draw conclusions about origins from inscriptions that are

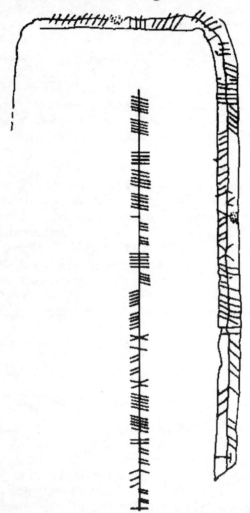

Figure Four An example of a Pictish Ogham inscription, as found on the edge of the Golspie Stone. The transliteration reads:

ALLHHALLORREDMEQQNIVVHRRERR
(Source: Close-Brooks, J, 1989)

as much as six hundred years later than Ptolemy's names and perhaps a thousand years after any postulated immigration. Languages can change rapidly when they are in close contact with others, and over such a long period. The Pictish invaders took Irish wives, so of course they would have introduced sound changes giving the language an Irish accent. Clearly the language would have absorbed many Irish names and loan words, so the recognition of some of these would not make it Goidelic. The proto-Picts were also in contact with Romans, the southern Britons and an aboriginal group; and their influences must also have penetrated the language.

As for whether the ogham-language was Finnic, well: Finnic languages are indeed non-Indo-European, but even if the various transliterations are accurate there is no way to know how they were pronounced. While it is possible to suggest *obvious* Finnic interpretations for some of Ptolemy's north-eastern names, the same may not be said of the oghams. That is not to say that a native Finno-Ugrian linguist would not find more success. Ptolemy's names suggest that any settlement must have occurred not long before the first century AD, and that divergence from the other Finnic languages had only just begun.

There can be no proof that the symbols found on the stones are the same as those that the Picts tattooed upon their faces and bodies. This, as Anthony Jackson suggests, must await the discovery of "a perfectly preserved bog Pict". Here again we may note the coincidence of the Baltic Aestii, who in addition to following Suebian fashions, also wore the symbol of the boar as emblem of the mother goddess, and in doing so put themselves under the personal protection of the goddess. The boar is indeed one of the Pictish symbols and this could be giving us a clue that they were each the totem of the ancestral god of a particular tribe or family. This custom occurred in some Finno-Ugrian tribes, whereby the image of the ancestral animal was placed in a shrine to which sacrifice was offered; and it was forbidden for a member of the tribe to kill the ancestral animal.[61]

The Baltic Finns were converted to Christianity in the twelfth century, but their pagan rites are known to have been similar to those of the Lapps, who were converted only as recently as the seventeenth and eighteenth centuries. A custom surviving among the Lapps was to set up idols of wood or stone

61   Hajdu, P (974), 132-134

called *seides,* which served as places of dedication and sacrifice.[62] The Lapps worshipped ancestor spirits and feared the actions of demons in every natural event; and every creature or even inanimate objects were believed to be possessed of a spirit. Their priests or shamans were known as *noaide.* They would attempt to placate the spirits by performing sacrifices or some other such rite at the seide, often assisted by a state of drug-induced trance.

The seide idols were typically set up in some place of natural power or atmosphere, for example: rock formations, caves, wells, or even the site of a lightning strike. The stone was considered to be the incarnation of the god to whom the seide was dedicated.

It is a small step from this to view the Pictish symbol stones as comparable sites of pagan dedication, endowed with the symbols of the deity to whom they were dedicated. This would explain why the symbols and the Christian cross sometimes occur together on the later stones, following the well-attested practice of the rededication of pagan shrines. Indeed some such form of worship may be intended in Joceline's Life of Kentigern, where the saint is said to have abolished "profane rites, almost equal to idolatry".

In the *Pictish Chronicle,* there is a note under the reign of the pre-historical king Nechtan Morbet that Abernethy was granted to Dairlugdach, Abbess of Kildare, as a monastic site of the Culdees. Skene translates: "Abernethy, with its territories, which are situated from the stone in Apurfeirt [*Apurfeirc*] to the stone beside Ceirfuill".[63] This would seem to attest to the use of stones to mark pagan religious territories; and indeed we know from the *Maen Gwyngwn* of the Gododdin that such territorial markers were used by the Picts. Why then should we not make the obvious connection with the symbol stones?

The association of many symbol stones with modern churches is also worth bearing in mind. If, as has been suggested here, the *Pit*-names represent converted Christian parishes then such continuity is to be expected. For example, the slab now housed in the church at Fordoun, holds one of the two inscriptions in Latin characters. It is usually read as: PIDARNOIN which, one may suggest, is the lost *Pit*-name of that parish.[64]

62   Vorren, O and Manker, E (1962), 121-7
63   Reeves, W (1864), 132
64   Diack, F C (1944), 76

The Pagan Religion of the Picts

Such positive details that we have of the Pictish religion come to us from the biased viewpoint of the early Christian saints and their later biographers; who were of course, most scathing of the old religion. The conversion of the northern Picts to Christianity is attributed to Saint Columba and later Saint Kentigern. Bede records that the southern Picts, or Miathi, had been converted rather earlier by the British monk Ninian, probably during the early fifth century.

The *Scotichronicon* records that the Picts, when first they came to this island, sacrificed to demons before they would engage in any action. The Pictish worship of demons, or disembodied spirits, is apparent in Adamnan's version of Columba's exorcism of a malevolent demon from a well or fountain, which the local Picts worshipped as a god. The cult of wells was well established elsewhere in Britain. Solinus records the dedication of hot springs to the goddess Minerva; although he does not positively associate this cult with those barbarians who tattooed themselves with animals, whom he describes a little further on in his narrative. A symbol stone with the crescent and V-rod symbols was found at a well near Dunvegan Castle on the Isle of Skye, which may indicate some pagan cult significance.

The Irish traditions of the origin of the Cruithni reveal a Druid named Drostan, who ordered them to bathe in cows milk as a form of magical protection. Saint Columba also encountered "Druids" in the territory of the northern Picts, who appeared to believe that their magical powers exceeded his own. His biographer Adamnan clearly did not differentiate them from Irish Druids, as he understood them.

St Ninian's biographer, Ailred, records that the Picts worshipped "deaf and dumb idols". Ninian operated from Whithorn, in Galloway, when it was still part of the independent north British kingdom. His see extended from Cumbria up to the Antonine wall, which was still the boundary of the Picts in his day. He evidently made an attempt to convert the southern Picts; Bede certainly accepted this, and an eighth century poem describes Ninian as visiting Picts who were called *Naturae*. Bede, in his *Life of Saint Cuthbert*, speaks of that saint's visit to "the land of the Picts who are called Niduari". The date of Cuthbert's visit falls in the period before the battle of Nechtansmere (Dunnichen) in 685 after which the Northumbrian Angles lost control of the southern Pictish province and the Bishop of the Picts fled from Abercorn (Peanfahel). The erection of the symbol stones dates from this period of renewed independence and may indicate a reassertion of northern Pictish culture at this era.

The assumption, certainly as far back as Bede and his anonymous source, has always been that these Niduari were a tribe or province of the southern Picts. Taken together with Bede's assertion that Ninian converted only the southern Picts, this assumption would place them somewhere between the central lowlands and the Mounth, but no tribe of this name is attested from any other source. Skene, in his *Celtic Scotland* believed the Niuduera region to be the Picts of Galloway.[65]

However, following the hypothesis that the Picts were Finnic, we may immediately see what is intended here. The *Niduari*, or *Niuduera*, were not a tribe of the Picts — but their Druids, who at that era may have been converted or lapsed Christians; and what is more likely than that a priest should visit the priests of the Picts? The word is clearly related to Finnish *noita* (Lappish: *noaida*, Estonian: *noid*) which means "magician" or "witch"; or more likely from *noitua* (Estonian: *noiduma*) meaning "to use magic" or "to bewitch". It seems that we have here preserved the Pictish word for a druid or a shaman, which may also have been retained as their name for a Christian priest.

65   Skene, W F (1876), vol 1, 212-3

Conclusions

The prevailing consensus that the Picts were Celts, and their language *p*-Celtic, rests heavily upon an interpretation of a few tribal and place names as Gallo-Brittonic; and upon the presence of a few apparently Celtic words within some late inscriptions. If doubt can be introduced into these assumptions then the entire Celtic hypothesis fails. It may be seen that a comparison of both place names and ethnic names with Finnish does yield some interesting results; and the degree of correspondence between the Finnic meaning of the names, the legends of Pictish origins, and the historical sources, is demanding of attention.

The tradition preserved by Bede and others would imply that the ancestors of the Picts were a maritime tribe from the Baltic; and their invasion must date from a prehistoric era, perhaps the first millennium BC. The legends say that they took wives from among the Scots of Ireland and that many Scots came over with them to Britain; so clearly the Picts were of mixed race from the outset. The apparent presence of Irish loan words in later Pictish sources, such as the ogham inscriptions, is therefore to be expected.

The presence of British elements in north-east place-names can also be readily explained, even if the Caledonii were not themselves Celts. In pre-Roman times the central lowlands were occupied by the Brythonic Damnonii, after whom Dumbarton is named. The building of the Antonine Wall arbitrarily divided their territory and the British speakers isolated north of the wall were driven northward by the punitive campaigns of Severus. The early conversion of the southern Picts to

Christianity must also have introduced influence from the Britons of Strathclyde. As we have seen above, none of Ptolemy's north-eastern names can be convincingly demonstrated as Celtic and there is nothing to prove that any *p*-Celtic place-names existed in north-east Scotland prior to the Roman campaigns.

It is perhaps understandable that the question of Pictish origins should have been examined so often by Gaelic Scots and Celtic specialists; and that they should have convinced themselves that the Picts and their forerunners were also Celts. This theory conveniently ignores the fact that many of the earliest ethnic names supplied by Ptolemy and the Roman authors for north-east Scotland have defied a Celtic interpretation. Many of the earliest names in the Pictish king lists are clearly not Celtic either; and the few arguably Celtic words found in the ogham inscriptions are all embedded within long and indecipherable agglutinations. It is inevitable that a non-Indo-European language, isolated in an insular context, would have absorbed numerous loan words from the neighbouring Celtic and other aboriginal languages, long before any of these written sources were set down.

The balance of evidence suggests that at least one of the languages spoken in the Pictish region, in pre and proto-Pictish times, was a Finno-Ugrian language closely related to modern Finnish and Estonian. However, even if one were to identify the Maeatae as these intrusive Finns, this still would not imply that the northern Caledonii and Taexali spoke the same language; still less the western tribes, such as the Creones and Cerones of Ptolemy.

Ethnically, the proto-Picts may be divided into three broad groupings. The first may be seen as a northern Celtic-speaking people who probably spoke a British dialect; and who are represented by the Caledonii and by the west-coast tribes on Ptolemy's map: the Creones, Cerones and Epidii; and possibly also the northern Cornovii and Smertae. They were collectively known to the Irish as Cruithni and to themselves simply as Priteni, "Britons". Some of these tribes may have been recent refugees from the Roman south. Others may represent aboriginal groups who had only recently lost their ancient language; and whose customs therefore preserved the aboriginal way of life that had prevailed throughout Britain in pre-Celtic times. As such, we should hesitate to call them Celts.

The second grouping is identifiable as one or more warlike aboriginal tribes of unknown association, represented at various times as Taexali, Verturiones and Attacotti; and in Irish sources by the warlike clans of Cait, Ce and Cirig. These aborigines probably lived in the north-east of Scotland, the western highlands and the Hebridean islands; all of which became absorbed into northern Pictish territory in historical times. As we encounter them in the Roman annals they are in the process of losing their independence; and in such circumstances, by analogy with the later Scottish absorption of the Picts, it is likely that their language and customs were suppressed. Perhaps something of them does survive in the title *Brude* and in other early names in the king lists; in the matrilineal succession; and in the polygamous practices that we find associated with all the northern tribes.

The third group may be seen as the true "Picts". These were an intrusive Finnic-Scythian tribe who settled both in Britain and in Ireland. We first meet them in the historical record as the Orcadians and as the Boresti, allies of Agricola. They next occur as Ptolemy's Venicones. Later still, as their alliance with Rome dissolved, we find them as the Maeatae, who became the dominant element within the later Pictish nation. As late as the sixth century Adamnan in his life of Saint Columba still refers to "Miathi", who are clearly the same as the Maeatae of Dio Cassius; and on the evidence of Bede, the later Pictish kingdom still retained this division between "northern" and "southern" Picts. It was they who introduced the Scythian custom of tattooing the body; and as a symbol of rank and status it came to be adopted by their subject tribes. They may have raided Britain originally as slave traders and remained as a warrior aristocracy. As they were all males they had no option but to integrate and absorb the customs of the aborigines.

It is no longer good enough to simply dismiss the tradition that the Picts were of "Scythian" origin. However, on balance, it seems that these legends are best reserved for an intrusive maritime element represented by the Orcadians, the southern Venicones and the Maeatae. They first absorbed the other southern tribes and later the Caledonii and Taexali of the north. The Romans applied the collective name of "Picts" (Latin *pictus* — "painted") to this troublesome confederation.

It is possible that names such as Caledonii, Taexali and Verturiones are merely those applied to these tribes by the southern Maeatae who, living nearest the Roman wall, had transmitted these names to the Romans during a period when they were allies of Rome. It is therefore understandable that Ptolemy's map should reflect military concerns. While we have a few indicators that the Caledonii may have been Celts, we have no firm information about the language and ethnic associations of the Taexali. However, from their names alone, we should not rule out the possibility that the older inhabitants were also of Finno-Ugrian descent, with closely related language and customs.

By the eighth century when Bede wrote, these groups were culturally and linguistically well mixed; we must accept his statement that by the historical period there was only a single Pictish nation and a single language. The evidence of the late names "Peanfahel" and "Niuduera" would argue that the language of the Maeatae had prevailed over the others and that later Pictish remained grammatically Finnic to the end. The question of Pictish origins would therefore benefit from a closer examination by specialists in the field of Finno-Ugrian etymology.

As to whether this hypothesis could answer all the questions about the Picts and their origins, I somehow doubt it. It simply raises a further series of questions. Whomsoever would wish to answer those had best go back and re-examine the Pictish sources.

The Historical Sources

The Historical Sources

The best way to study history is always from the sources. On the subject of Pictish origins this is particularly important, as the weight of learned discussion can sometimes give the impression that there is a great body of evidence available to specialists; whereas in truth, there are but a few unsatisfactory references, of which fewer still are by authors contemporary with the events.

Since I have collected these translated extracts for my own use, they are published here for the benefit of others; and so that the reader may easily review the relevant literary authorities before pursuing them back to text. A difficulty then arises as to which references should be included and which excluded. I have tried to limit the selection to only those fragments that directly allude to the proto-Picts, or later works that throw some light on their ethnic origin, customs and language. I have also included a number of more imprecise references to British tribes and customs, which may, in their generality, encompass the northern tribes. I have entirely omitted any references to the historical Pictish period, or to the early Scots, for which there is ample coverage in other works.

The extracts are in chronological order of the authors rather than of the events described. Any italics within square brackets are by the present author.

Julius Caesar (54 BC)[1]

The Gallic War V, 12
The interior of Britain is inhabited by tribes who claim, on the strength of an oral tradition, to be aboriginal; the coast by Belgic invaders who came to plunder...

V, 14
...Most of the tribes in the interior do not grow corn, but live on milk and meat, and wear skins. All the Britons dye their bodies with woad, which produces a blue colour, and shave the whole of their bodies except the head and upper lip. Wives are shared between groups of ten or twelve men, especially between brothers and between fathers and sons; but the offspring of these unions are counted as the children of the man with whom a particular woman cohabited first.

There can be no certainty that Caesar's references to the tribes in the interior of Britain are relevant to the northern tribes — but equally there is no evidence that they are not. Compare the marriage customs described by Caesar with the free association of Caledonian women reported by Dio Cassius, and with the matrilineal succession of the later Picts.

Diodorus Siculus (c 30 BC)[2]

Library of History V, 21, 3
Britain is triangular in shape...and the last, [cape] writers tell us, extends out into the open sea and is named Orca[s].

V, 21, 5
And Britain, we are told, is inhabited by tribes which are autochthonous and preserve in their ways of living the ancient manner of life. They use chariots, for instance...

1   Handford, S A, *Caesar - The Conquest of Gaul* (Penguin, Harmondsworth, 1951)
2   Oldfather, C H, *Diodorus Siculus*, Vol 3 (Harvard University Press, Cambridge, Massachusets 1993)

Strabo (c 7 BC)[3]

Geography IV, 5, 3
[*On the lack of any commercial justification for an invasion of Britain.*]
At present, however, some of the chieftains there, after procuring the friendship of Caesar Augustus by sending embassies and by paying court to him...have managed to make the whole of the island virtually Roman property.

If this statement were to be taken literally it would have to imply trading contact with the northern tribes also; and might support the belief of some later authors, such as Eutropius, that the Orkneys submitted immediately to the invasion of Claudius.

Lucan (AD 39-65)[4]

Civil Wars VI, 67-8
[*In the context that Pompey failed to notice Caesar's fortifications*]
...Or when the tides of Ocean and the Rutupian shore are raging, the stormy waves are not heard by the Caledonian Britons.

Pliny the Elder (AD 77)[5]

Natural History, IV, xvi, 102
...nearly thirty years ago its exploration was carried by the armed forces of Rome to a point not beyond the neighbourhood of the Caledonian Forest.

This was written only a few years *before* the circumnavigation by Agricola's fleet and, according to various later writers, some thirty years *after* the Orkneys had supposedly already submitted to Claudius. Pliny describes forty

3   Jones, H L, *The Geography of Strabo* (Harvard University Press, Cambridge, Massachusets, 1988)
4   Duff, J D, *Lucan - The Civil War (Pharsalia)* (Harvard University Press, Cambridge, Massachusets, 1928)
5   Rackham, H, *Pliny - Natural History*, Vol 2 (Harvard University Press, Cambridge, Massachusets, 1989)

Orcades islands; and other islands: *Dumna* (Lewis or Harris), *Bergi* and *Berrice* (probably inner Hebridean islands); and seven *Acmodae* islands (probably the Shetlands), mistakenly identified as Thule by Agricola's fleet.

Tacitus (AD 98)[6]

Agricola 10
[His description of Britain]
...when you go further north you find a large and shapeless tract of country, jutting out to form what is actually the most distant coastline and finally tapering into a kind of wedge. These remotest shores were now circumnavigated, for the first time, by a Roman fleet, which thus established the fact that Britain was an island. At the same time it discovered and subjugated the Orkney Islands, hitherto unknown. Thule too, was sighted, but no more; their orders took them no further and winter was close at hand...

11
Who the first inhabitants *[of Britain]* were, whether natives or immigrants, is open to question: one must remember we are dealing with barbarians. But their physical characteristics vary, and the variation is suggestive. The reddish hair and large limbs of the Caledonians proclaim a German origin; the swarthy faces of the Silures, the tendency for their hair to curl, and the fact that Spain lies opposite, all lead one to believe that Spaniards crossed in ancient times and occupied that part of the country. The peoples nearest Gaul likewise resemble them. It may be that they still show the effect of a common origin; or perhaps it is climatic conditions that have produced this physical type in lands that converge so close in their shores. In both countries you find the same ritual and religious beliefs. There is no great difference in language, and there is the same...

6   Mattingley, H, *Tacitus - the Agricola and the Germania* (Penguin, Harmondsworth, 1989)

25

In the summer in which his sixth year of office began, Agricola enveloped the tribes beyond the Forth. Fearing a general rising of the northern nations and threatening movements by the enemy on land, he used his fleet to reconnoitre the harbours...The natives of Caledonia turned to armed resistance on a large scale - though the facts were exaggerated...

29

[*On the campaign of the seventh year*]
...He sent his fleet ahead to plunder at various points and thus spread uncertainty and terror; then, with an army marching light, which he had reinforced by some of the bravest of the Britons who had proved their loyalty by long years of submission, he reached Mount Graupius, which he found occupied by the enemy. The Britons were, in fact, undaunted by the loss of the previous battle, and were, ready for either revenge or enslavement. They had realised at last that the common danger must be warded off by united action, and had sent round embassies and drawn up treaties to rally the full force of their states. Already more that 30,000 men could be seen, and still they came flocking to the colours — all the young men and famous warriors whose "old age was fresh and green", every man bearing the decorations he had earned. At that point one of the many leaders, a man of outstanding valour and nobility named Calgacus addressed the close-packed multitude of men...[*There follow speeches by Calgacus and Agricola, and an account of the battle, which supply little useful ethnic detail.*]

Diack (1944) suggested that the description of every man bearing his decorations or arms may be a reference to tattooing.

38

...As the summer was almost over, it was impossible for operations to be extended over a wider area; so Agricola led his army into the territory of the Boresti. There he took hostages and ordered his admiral to sail round the north of Britain...

Martial (AD 86-94)[7]

Epigrams X, 44
Quintus Ovidius, you are going to visit the Caledonian Britons...

XI, 53
Claudia Rufina sprang from the Blue Britons...

XIV, 97
I have come, a barbarian basket, from the painted Britons...

Vindolanda Tablet II 164 (c AD 100-117)[8]

...the Britons are unprotected by armour. There are very many cavalry. The cavalry do not use swords nor do the "wretched little Brits" [Brittunculi] mount in order to throw javelins.

This is one of the inscriptions on wooden tablets found at Vindolanda (Chesterholm) on Hadrian's Wall in 1973; and dating from the early period of the Stanegate frontier.

Juvenal (AD 105)[9]

II, 160-1
We have pushed beyond the shores of Ireland [Iuvernae], and newly captured Orkneys [Orcadas] and those content with the briefest night, the Britons.

Pausanias (c AD 140)[10]

The Description of Greece VIII, C, 43
...and he [Antoninus] deprived the Brigantes of Britain of a great portion of their land, because, with arms,

7   Shackleton-Bailey, D R, *Martial-Epigrams* (Harvard University Press, Cambridge, Massachusets, 1993)
8   Potter, T W, *Roman Britain* (British Museum Press, London, 1997)
9   Robinson, S, *Juvenal - Sixteen Satires upon the Ancient Harlot* (Carcanet New Press, Manchester, 1983)
10   Petrie, H, *Monumenta Historica Britannica* (London, 1848 [reprinted 1969])

they had begun to overrun the territory of the Genuini, who were tributary to the Romans.

No tribe named the *Genuini* are otherwise known in Britain. The Brigantes held territory in northern England and Scotland up to the Southern Uplands; and a tribe of the same name also lived in Ireland. The Genuini may therefore have been a northern frontier tribe to which Pausanias has applied the wrong name. One is reminded here of the *Gwyngwn* implied in the Gododdin, which J T Koch (1986) believed to be a British or old Welsh rendering of Ptolemy's name *Venicones*.

Ptolemy (c AD 150)[11]

Geography, C, liii
Geography of the British island Alvion
The description of the north side, above which is the Ocean called Duecaledonius:

	Long		**Lat**	
Peninsula of the Novantae and Cape of the same name	21		61	40
Rerigonius Bay	20	30	60	50
Vindogara Bay	21	20	60	30
Estuary of Clota	22	15	59	20
Lemannonius Gulf	21		60	
Cape Epidium	23		60	40
Mouth of the river Longus	21	30	60	40
Mouth of the river Itys	27		60	40
Volas Bay	29		60	30
Mouth of the river Nabarus	30		60	30
Tarvedum or Orcas Cape	31	20	60	15

The description of the west side, to which are adjacent both the Ivernic Ocean and the Vergionius Ocean. After the Cape of the Novantae:

Mouth of the river Abravannus	19	20	61	
Estuary of Iena	19		60	30
Mouth of the river Deva	18		60	
Mouth of the river Novius	18	20	59	30
Estuary of Ituna	18	30	58	45

11 MacBain, A, 'Ptolemy's Geography of Scotland', *Transactions of the Gaelic Society of Inverness*, 21 (1891-92), 191-214

The description of the next sides looking south-east, to which is adjacent the Germanic Ocean. After Cape Tarvedum or Orcas, which has been mentioned:

	Long		Lat	
Cape Virvedrum	31		60	
Cape Verubium	30	30	59	40
Mouth of the river Ila	30		59	40
High Bank	29		59	40
Estuary of Varar	27		59	40
Mouth of the river Loxa	27	30	59	40
Estuary of Tuesis	27		59	
Mouth of the river Caelis	27		58	45
Cape of the Taezali [Taexali]	27	30	58	30
Mouth of the river Deva	26		58	30
Estuary of Tava	25		58	50
Mouth of the river Tina	24		58	30
Estuary of Boderia	22	30	59	
Mouth of the river Alaunus	21	20	58	30
Mouth of the river Vedra	20	10	58	30

[*There follows here Ptolemy's description of southern Scotland, in which he describes the Novantae, Selgovae, Damnonii and Otadini (or Votadini); together with their various cities. He then moves on to describe the northern tribes.*]

After the Damnonii towards the east, but more northerly, from Cape Epidium about eastwards are the Epidii, after whom (the Cerones, then more easterly) the Creones, then the Carnonacae, then the Caereni, and, most easterly and furthest, the Cornavii. From the Lemannonius Gulf as far as the estuary of Varar are the Caledonii and above them the Caledonian Forest; from them more easterly are the Decantae, touching whom are the Lugi, and above the Lugi are the Smertae. Below the Caledonii are the Vacomagi among whom are these towns:

Bannatia	24		59	30
Tamia	25		59	20
Alata Castra				
(Winged Camp)	27	15	59	20
Tuesis	26	45	29	10

Below these but more westerly are the Venicones, among whom is this town:

	Long	Lat	
Orrea	24	58	45

More easterly are the Taezali [Taexali] and their city:

	Long	Lat
Devana	26	59

Variant forms of Ptolemy's names may be found in the *Monumenta Historica Britannica* which translates a Greek text. The most significant variants listed there are: *Venicontes* (Venicones), *Mertae* (Smertae), *Logi* (Lugi) and *Cantae* (Decantae).

Ptolemy's ethnic descriptions are difficult to interpret without an appreciation of the related geography. Reconstructions of the map from the latitude and longitude tables show a curious map of Britain with Scotland turned through a right angle. Ptolemy took his geography from an earlier atlas by Marinus of Tyre (known only from Ptolemy's own references) and it is evident that Marinus took his detail of northern and southern Britain from two quite separate maps. Once this error is corrected the description becomes recognisable — although some place names remain problematic; for "north" and "south" read west and east respectively; for "west" and "east" similarly read south and north. This mapping error was persistent! Therefore when presented with later reports of Picts "from the north", we should bear in mind that the north west coast and islands may be intended.

The era of Marinus was c AD 100-120 and this probably explains why no detail of either the wall of Hadrian or Antoninus is shown. Pliny's earlier geography of AD 77 indicates that nothing was yet known of Caledonia; the cities indicated must therefore reflect the early series of forts built by Agricola and his immediate successors. It has been suggested [*Rivett & Smith (1979), p193*] that Marinus, Ptolemy and also the later *Ravenna Cosmography* (c AD 700) all took their information from a military map dating from the Flavian period. The Ravenna Cosmography, since it is of such a late date, can scarcely be regarded as a reliable source of information about the proto-Picts. Indeed Ravenna lists many of Ptolemy's tribes as place names.

Ptolemy's description of the west coast is entirely devoid of cities, showing a succession of tribes from Epidium

Promontorium (The Mull of Kintyre) to Cape Orcas (Dunnet Head). The Caledonii are located centrally in the Great Glen, between the Lemannonius Gulf (Loch Long) and the Varar estuary (Beauly Firth). This identification forces the Decantae, Lugi and Smertae north of Inverness.

The interpretation of the eastern side is dependent upon an identification of the cities with Roman forts. Four are listed in the territory of the Vacomagi, and these may indicate the camps along Strathmore and the Mearns. The Taexali are therefore to be located above them in Aberdeenshire, as far as Taexalorum Promontorium (Kinnairds Head), with the Venicones below them in Fife and Gowrie.

Dio Cassius (before AD 229) in Xiphilinus Epitome of 11th Century AD[12]

Roman History
Epitome of Book LXXV, 5, 4
[*In AD 197 the Caledonians have apparently broken an earlier treaty*]
In as much as the Caledonians did not abide by their promises and had made ready to aid the Maeatae, and in view of the fact that Severus at the time was devoting himself to the neighbouring war, Lupus was compelled to purchase peace from the Maeatae for a large sum; and he received a few captives.

LXXVII, 12, 1-4
[*On the AD 208-11 campaign of Severus*]
There are two principal tribes of the Britons, the Caledonii and the Maeatae, and the names of the others have been merged in these two. The Maeatae live next to the cross-wall which cuts the island in half, and the Caledonians are beyond them. Both tribes inhabit wild and waterless mountains and desolate swampy plains, and possess neither walls, cities, nor tilled fields, but live on their flocks, wild game, and certain fruits; for they do not touch the fish which are found in immense and inexhaustible quantities. They dwell in tents, naked and unshod, possess their women in common and in common rear all their offspring. Their form of

12   Cary, E *Dio Cassius*, Vol 9 (Harvard University Press, Cambridge, Massachusets, 1982)

rule is democratic for the most part, and they are fond of plundering; consequently they choose their boldest men as rulers. They go into battle in chariots, and have small swift horses; there are also foot soldiers, very swift in running and very firm in standing their ground. For arms they have a shield and a short spear, with a bronze apple attached to the end of the spear-shaft, so that when it is shaken it may clash and terrify the enemy; and they also have daggers. They can endure hunger and cold and any kind of hardship; for they plunge into the swamps and exist there for many days with only their heads above water, and in the forests they support themselves upon bark and roots, and for all emergencies they prepare a certain kind of food, the eating of a small portion of which, the size of a bean, prevents them from feeling either hunger or thirst...

LXXVII, 13,1-4
Severus, accordingly, desiring to subjugate the whole of it, invaded Caledonia...[*there follows an account of the hardship endured by the Roman soldiers*]...But Severus did not desist until he had approached the extremity of the island...Having been conveyed through practically the whole of the hostile country (for he was conveyed in a covered litter most of the way, on account of his infirmity), he returned to the friendly portion after he had forced the Britons to come to terms on the condition that they should abandon a large part of their territory.

LXXVII, 15,1-2
When the inhabitants of the island again revolted, he summoned the soldiers and ordered them to invade the rebels' country, killing everybody they met; and he quoted these words: [*there follows a quotation from Homer*].

...When this had been done, and the Caledonians had joined the revolt of the Maeatae, he began preparing to make war upon them in person. [*there follows an account of the death of Severus shortly after this*].

LXXVII, 16, 5
[*in the context of some new laws to be introduced at Rome regarding adultery*]
In this connection, a very witty remark is reported to have been made by the wife of Argentocoxus, a Caledonian, to Julia Augusta. When the empress was jesting with her, after the treaty, about the free intercourse of her sex with men in Britain, she replied: "we fulfil the demands of nature in a much better way than do you Roman women; for we consort openly with the best men, whereas you let yourselves be debauched in secret by the vilest." Such was the retort of the British woman.

Herodian (before AD 238)[13]

History of Rome III, 14, 4
[*On the 208-11 campaign of Severus*]
Disconcerted by the emperor's sudden arrival, and realising that this huge army had been assembled to make war upon them, the Britons sent envoys to Severus to discuss terms of peace, anxious to make amends for their previous errors.

III, 14, 6-8
Most of the regions of Britain are marshy, since they are continually flooded by the tides of the ocean; the barbarians are accustomed to swimming or wading through these waist-deep marsh pools; since they go about naked, they are unconcerned at muddying their bodies. Strangers to clothing, the Britons wear ornaments of iron at their waists and throats; considering iron a symbol of wealth, they value this metal as other barbarians value gold. They tattoo their bodies with coloured designs and drawings of all kinds of animals; for this reason they do not wear clothes, which would conceal the decorations on their bodies. Extremely savage and warlike, they are armed only with a spear and a narrow shield, plus a sword that hangs suspended by a belt from their otherwise naked bodies. They do not use breast-plates or helmets, considering them encumbrances in crossing the marshes. For all these reasons...

13   Echols, E C H, *Herodian of Antioch* (Univ of California, 1961)

Inscription from a tablet found at Colchester (AD 222-235)[14]

> To Mars Medocius, god of the Campenses, and to the victory of our Emperor Alexander, pius, felix, as a gift at his own expense from Lossio Veda, a Caledonian, sister's son of Vepogenus.

In the opinion of J T Koch (1980) the name Vepogenus means "Fife-born".

Solinus (c AD 250)[15]

[The following extract is taken from the translation of the "Polyhistor" made by Arthur Golding in 1587. I have not deigned to modernise his Elizabethan English, which remains perfectly clear.]

> Collectanea Rerum Memorabilium, additamenta, 22, (11-17)
> ...For it is in length eyght hundred myles and more, so we measure it to the angle of Calydon [*Calidoniae*]...There bee many other iles about Brytaine, of which Thule [*Tylen*] is y furthest...From the promontorie of Calydon, to the Iland Thule, is two days sayling. Beyond Thule is the dead and frozen sea. Next come the iles called Hebudes [*Ebudes*] five in number, the inhabitants whereof, know not what corne meaneth but live onely by fishe and milke. They are all undere the government of one king, for as many of them as bee, they are severed but with a narrow groope one from another. The king hath nothing of hys own, but taketh from every mans. Hee is bound to equitie by certaine lawes: and lest he may start from right through covetousness, he learneth justice by povertie, as who may have nothing proper or peculiar to himselfe, but is found at the charges of the Realme. Hee is not suffered to have anie woman to himselfe, but whomsoever he hath minde unto, he borroweth for a tyme, and so others by turnes. Whereby it comes to passe that he hath neither desire nor hope of issue.

14 Diack, F C, *The Inscriptions of Pictland*, Spalding Club, Aberdeen, 1944
15 Golding A, *Solinus - Collectanea Rerum Memorabilium* (1587, reprinted in facsimile by Scholars Facsimiles and Reprints, Gainsville, Florida, 1955)

The second harborough between the maine lande and the Hebuds, is the Orcades: which are fró the Hebuds seven dayes and as manie nyghts sayling...[*continuing with a description of Thule and the Orkneys*]...They use their women in common, and no manne hath any wife.

Collectanea Rerum Memorabilium, 22, 12 (20)
[*Describing the mainland of Britain*]
...The Realme is partlie inhabited of barbarous people, who even fró theyr childhoode have shapes of divers beastes cunninglye impressed and incorporate in theyr bodyes, so that beeing engraved in theyr bowels, as the man groweth, so growe the marks painted upon him, neyther do those nations count any thing almost to be a greater token of patience, then y bodyes shoulde by manifest scarres drinke in the deepest colour.

The remarks on Hebridean customs are believed to be additions made by an Irish interpolator [*Zimmer (1898) p 26-28*] after AD 600 when the work was revised under the title *Polyhistor*. The reference to Britain being "partly inhabited" by a tribe who tattooed their bodies, must therefore imply the northern part. It is also worthy of note that the islanders are *not* described as tattooing their bodies. Here, the Hebrides implies the inner islands only; and Thule, in Solinus at least, appears to be Lewis or all of the long island, as may be deduced from the fact that all the islanders exhibit similar customs; and since it is described as only two days sailing from Caithness, yet seven days are required from Hebrides to Orkney. Solinus drew some ninety per cent of his material from Pliny. Solinus in turn was relied upon heavily by Isidore of Seville in his *Etymologiae*.

Oppian (third century)[16]

Cygnetica I, 468-80
...These [*hunting dogs*] the wild tribes of Britons, with their tattooed backs, rear and call by the name of Agassian.

16 Ireland, S, *Roman Britain - A Sourcebook* (London, Second Edition, 1996)

Other translators of this passage give "painted Britons". The breeding of dogs in Britain is also discussed by Nemesianus: Cygnetica, 225f; and by Claudian: Stilicho III, 301.

Scriptores Historiae Augustae (various authors, late third century)[17]

[Translation from the text of H Petrie]

> Antoninus Pius V
> Using his governors Antoninus waged many wars. In Britain, through the governor Lollius Urbicus he drove back the barbarians and built another wall, this time of turf.

The above is an example of a number of references by the authors of the *Historia Augusta* to wars on the northern frontier during the second century AD, in this case initiating the building of the northern wall. Unfortunately all the references are vague about the barbarians themselves. Other references under Hadrian V and XI refer to wars in Britain and to the building of the southern wall (AD 117-122); Marcus Aurelius VIII, 7 and XXII, 2 mention an uprising in AD 163.

Panegyric of Constantius (AD 297)[18]

> XI
> [*Comparing the achievements of Constantius to the task that had faced Julius Caesar*]
> ...and the Britons, a nation still then primitive and accustomed only to the half-naked Picts and Hibernians as their sole enemies, who gave way easily to Roman arms...

Smythe in *Warlords and Holy Men*, p 52, points out that this, the earliest reference to Picts by that name, implies their presence also in the time of Julius Caesar and indeed earlier; and suggests that the use of the term "proto-Picts" prior to this date should be regarded as a wholly artificial division.

---

17 Petrie, H, *Monumenta Historica Britannica* (London, 1848 [reprinted 1969])
18 Galletier, E, *Panegyrici Latini* (Paris 1949)

63

Panegyric of Constantine (AD 310)[19]

> VII
> [*In reference to the expedition of his father Constantius to Britain in AD 306*]
> In his last campaign he did not seek any British trophies...I do not speak of the woods and marshes of the Caledones and other Picts, still less nearby Ireland or farthest Thule...

Some translators of this passage give an alternative: "Caledones, Picts and others". It is clearly important to establish whether or not the Caledonians were Picts. The Latin is: *Neque enim ille tot tantisque rebus gestis non dico Caledonum aliorumque Pictorum siluas et paludes, sed nec Hiberniam proximam nec Thylem ultimam...* The context after all, is a poem, with all due licence.

Eusebius (before AD 340)[20]

> The Life of Constantine I, c, 8
> [*On the expedition of Constantine to Britain in AD 313*]
> And having fortified his army with the mild and pure precepts of religion, he went against the land of the Britons, and against those who dwell in that ocean which is bounded by the setting sun.
>
> I, c, 25
> ...Contemplating the remaining portions of the habitable earth, he then passed over to the British nations, lying within the very ocean: and having subjugated these, he turned his mind to the other parts of the world.
> IV, c, 50
> And during his reign the Britons within the western ocean were first subdued.

Britain had been part of the empire for two and a half centuries by the reign of Constantine. The reference to his British campaign may therefore imply an expedition to the west of Scotland and the islands.

19   Galletier, E, *Panegyrici Latini* (Paris 1949)
20   Petrie, H, *Monumenta Historica Britannica* (London, 1848 [reprinted 1969])

Eutropius (AD 360)[21]

[Translation from the text of H Petrie]

Summary of Roman History   VII, 13, 3
[*On the Claudian invasion of Britain in AD 43*]
...He added to the Roman Empire the islands in the
ocean beyond Britain called the Orchades.

For the truth of this matter see also Strabo, Pliny and Tacitus.
Later authors follow Eutropius.

Ammianus Marcellinus (AD 330-395)[22]

Library of History, XXVII, 7, 8
When the Picts, Attacotti and Scots, after killing a
general and a count, were devastating Britain without
resistance, Count Theodosius routed them and took
their booty from them.

XXVII, 8, 5
It will, however, be in place to say that at that time the
Picts, divided into two tribes, called Dicalydones and
Verturiones, as well as the Attacotti, a warlike race of
men, and the Scots, were ranging widely and causing
great devastation; while the Gallic regions, wherever
anyone could break in by land or sea, were harassed
by the Franks and their neighbours, the Saxons...

Theodosius appears to have pursued the Picts all the way
back to the Caledonian Forest, as recorded by Claudian,
probably in 368 or 369.

21 Petrie, H, *Monumenta Historica Britannica* (London, 1848 [reprinted 1969])
22 Rolfe, J C, *Ammianus Marcellinus*, vol III (Harvard University Press,
    Cambridge, Massachusets, 1939)

Vegetius Renatus (fourth century)[23]

[Translation from the text of H Petrie]

> Summary of Military Affairs, IV, 37
> [*Describing the interception of enemy vessels by Roman scout ships*]
> ...these [*scout boats*] are called by the Britons *Pictas*. They are intended to locate and occasionally intercept the enemy ships, or to observe their movements. However, so that these scout-boats are not bright and easily visible, their sails, rigging, and even the wax with which they are covered, are camouflaged in a sea-green colour.

Although the context is clearly Britain, nothing here proves that the sea-borne raiders are Picts; the raiders could as easily be Saxon or Irish. Chadwick (1958) has suggested that the name of the boats (variants: *Picatos*, *Pictos*) may intend a pun on picti or "painted".

Claudian (c 400AD) Panegyrics to Various Emperors[24]

> The Gothic War, 415-420
> ...next the legion that had kept the fierce Scots in check, whose men had scanned the strange devices tattooed on the faces of the dying Picts...

> On Stilicho's Consulship, II, 247-255
> Next spoke Britain clothed in the skin of some Caledonian beast, her cheeks tattooed, and an azure cloak, rivalling the swell of ocean, sweeping to her feet: "Stilicho gave aid to me also when at the mercy of neighbouring tribes, what time the Scots roused all Hibernia against me and the sea foamed to the beat of hostile oars. Thanks to his care I had no need to fear the Scottish arms or tremble at the Picts, or keep watch all along my coasts for the Saxon who might come whatever wind might blow."

23 Petrie, H, *Monumenta Historica Britannica* (London, 1848 [reprinted 1969])
24 Platnauer, M, *Claudian* (Harvard University Press, Cambridge, Massachusets, 1922)

The Fourth Consulship of Honorius, 25-33
Hence came Theodosius, grandfather of
Honorius...'Twas he who pitched his camp amid the
snows of Caledonia...brought into subjection the coasts
of Britain and with equal success laid waste the north
and the south. What avail against him the eternal
snows, the frozen air, the uncharted sea? The Orcades
ran red with Saxon slaughter; Thule was warm with
the blood of Picts; ice-bound Hibernia wept for the
heaps of slain Scots.

Against Eutropius, I, 390-293
...The Saxon is conquered and the seas safe; the Picts
have been defeated and Britain is secure.

Stilicho appears to have been active against the Picts and
Scots around AD 395, but his precise achievements go
unrecorded.

St Jerome(c AD 393)[25]

[Translation from the text of J P Migne]

Against Jovinian, 2, 7
...To these may be added similar [*meat-eating*] tribes.
I myself, when a youth in Gaul, recall the Atticoti, a
British tribe, who eat human flesh. They lived in the
forests and were adept at tearing-off the breasts of the
daughters and wives of the shepherds and pig farmers
— and considered them a delicacy. The race of Scots
do not have wives as we understand them, but as in
Plato's state...

A regiment of the Attacotti (here: "Atecotti") are listed in
the *Notitia Dignitatum* or "List of Offices" at about AD 400 as
being stationed in Italy and Gaul; some 20-30 years after the
period when Jerome might have encountered them as a youth
in Gaul. Jerome's is the only report that might indicate some
kind of cannibalistic practice among the northern British tribes,
but it is not entirely clear whether the Atticoti are Scots recently
settled in Britain, since Jerome speaks of both as having similar
customs.

25   Migne, J P, *Patrologia Latina*, vols XXII & XXIII (1844)

Epistola 69 (written c AD 400)
[*Jerome likens the sins of his converts to the promiscuous practices of the Scots and Atticoti*]...the novices who bring their children to baptism do not even enter into honourable marriages; but like the Scots and the Atticoti, or as in Plato's Republic, they allow their brides to be promiscuous and live together freely in communes;...

The report of the free association of the Atticotti women is not unlike that ascribed to aboriginal Britons by Caesar; to the Maeatae and to the wife of the Caledonian Argentocoxus by Dio Cassius; and apparently it was also a custom of the Scots. The inhabitants of the Inner Hebrides, according to Solinus, followed similar social practices and surely we need look no further to identify who the Atticotti were. Jerome sees their social customs as similar to those discussed in books V-VII of Plato's *Republic*. However, whereas Plato envisaged that the rulers of his ideal state would decide who should procreate, rather it is clear from Dio Cassius that the British women had complete freedom of association.

Saint Patrick (c 450)[26]

Epistola 2
...Like the enemy they live in death, as allies of Irish [*Scots*] and of Picts and apostates...

12
...Far from God's love is the man who delivers Christians into the hands of Irish and Picts...

15
...Therefore the church mourns and weeps for its sons and daughters who have not so far been put to the sword, but have been carried off and transported to distant lands, where sin is rife, openly, grievously and shamelessly; and where freeborn men have been sold, Christians reduced to slavery — and what is more, as slaves of the utterly iniquitous, evil and apostate Picts.

26 Hood, A B, *Saint Patrick - His Writings and Muirchu's Life* (Phillimore, London, 1978)

68

The context is Patrick's open letter in condemnation of Coroticus, a king of the North Britons, who had been raiding Patrick's Irish converts and selling them as slaves to the Picts, and also to the heathen Scots. The reference to the Picts as "apostate" is usually taken to imply a lapse after some previous conversion. The location of the Picts cannot be determined and we cannot rule out that the reference here may be to Picts in Galloway.

The Gallic Chronicle of 452[27]

[*Prior to the rebellion of Magnus Maximus, Governor of Britain in 382*]
Maximus rapidly defeated the Picts and Scots who were making attacks.

Sidonius (c 455)[28]

Panegyric on Avitus VII, 88-91
Caesar took his victorious legions even to the Caledonian Britons, and although he routed the Scot, the Pict and the Saxon, he still looked for foes...

Constantius (fifth century AD)[29]

The Life of Saint Germanus 17
[*Germanus visits Britain in AD 429 to refute the heresy of Pelagius.*]
In the meantime, the Picts and Saxons joined forces and made war on the Britons...[*there follows an account of how Lupus routed the enemy by the singing of Alleluia.*]

The Annals of Clonmacnoise (see below) would make the Picts the enemy at this time.

27 Ireland, S, *Roman Britain - A Sourcebook* (London, Second Edition, 1996)
28 Anderson, W B, *Sidonius*, Vol 1 (Harvard University Press, Cambridge, Massachusets 1936)
29 Ireland, S, *Roman Britain - A Sourcebook* (London, Second Edition, 1996)

Gildas (c 540 AD)[30]

The Ruin of Britain, 14

After that, Britain was despoiled of her whole army [*by Maximus*]…Quite ignorant of the ways of war, she groaned aghast for many years, trodden under foot first by two exceedingly savage nations, the Scots from the north-west and the Picts from the north.

16

The legion returned home triumphant and joyful. Meanwhile the old enemies re-appeared, like greedy wolves, rabid with extreme hunger, who, dry-mouthed, leap over into the sheepfold when the shepherd is away. They came relying on their oars as wings, on the arms of their oarsman, and on the winds swelling their sails. They broke through the frontiers, spreading destruction everywhere. They went trampling over everything that stood in their path, cutting it down like ripe corn.

19 1-2

As the Romans went back home, there emerged from the coracles that had carried them across the sea-valleys the foul hordes of Scots and Picts, like dark throngs of worms who wriggle out of narrow fissures when the sun is high and the weather grows warm. They were to some extent different in their customs, but were in perfect accord in their greed for bloodshed: and they were readier to cover their villainous faces with hair than their private parts with clothes. They were more confident than usual now that they had learnt of the departure of our fellow debtors and the denial of any prospect of their return. So they seized the whole of the extreme north of the island from its inhabitants, right up to the wall. A force was stationed on the high towers to oppose them, but it was too lazy to fight, and too unwieldy to flee; the men were foolish and frightened and sat about day and night rotting away in their folly. Meanwhile there was no respite from the barbed spears flung by their naked opponents, which tore our wretched countrymen from the walls and

30 Winterbottom, M, *Gildas - The Ruin of Britain and other Documents* (Phillimore, London, 1978)

dashed them to the ground. Premature death was in fact an advantage to those who were snatched away; for their quick end saved them from the miserable fate that awaited their brothers and children.

21
...So the impudent Irish pirates returned home (though they were shortly to return); and for the first time the Picts in the far end of the island kept quiet from now on, though they occasionally carried out devastating raids of plunder.

Isidore of Seville (560-653)[31]

Etymologiae IX, ii, 103
The Scots, in their own language, are named from their painted bodies, perhaps a comment because they brand themselves with various figures using ink and an iron needle.

XIX, xxii, xxiii, 7-8
The race of the Picts are so named from their bodies, because a craftsman works on them with the point of a needle and the juice of a native wild grass, so that the scars are left as signs. Even those of noble birth are disfigured by painted limbs. Both sexes may display the custom, so that it is a mark of rank to cut-off excess hair; among women especially, they adorn themselves with the hair heaped-up, covering and circling the crown of the head like a head-dress.

As Skene noted, the tenth century "Pictish Chronicle" (which extensively quotes Isidore) substitutes "Picts" for "Scots" here. The reference to the elevating of the hair is similar to that which Tacitus ascribes to the Germanic Suebi, to give additional height.

---

31   Lindsay, W M, *Isidori Hispalensis Episcopi Etymologiarum sive Origines*, Vol 1 & II (Clarendon, Oxford, 1911)

Taliesin (late sixth century)[32]

[*An extract from Cadau Gwallwg from the Book of Taliesin*]
He is well known in Prydyn and Eiddin,
in Gafran and the land of Brychan,
in Erbin,
brave and caparisoned,
those who have not seen Gwallawg
have not seen a man.

An example of *Prydyn* as the name of the Picts in early Welsh sources. Gwallawg may be identified as a young prince who fought with Urien, king of the north Britons, against the Angles of Northumbria between 572 and 592. Apparently his fame had spread even to the Picts (Prydyn) living in Edinburgh and Brechin.

Aneirin (c AD 600)[33]

The Gododdin   B 13 = CA xxii B
...he was in charge of a hundred men, the noble warrior of renowned spirit, the foreign horseman, the young son of Cian from beyond Bannog. The men of Gododdin do not tell of anyone more harsh than Llifiau when he was on the field of battle.

The Gododdin   A9 = CA ix
...The brave man wanted no father-in-law's dowry, the young son of Cian from Maen Gwyngwn.

Among the elegies to the various warriors who died in battle against the Saxons at Catreath (Catterick) is this one to Llif or Llifiau, son of Cian. These two references show that the stone "Maen Gwyngwn" lay "beyond Bannog" and *Bannog* implies the Fintry Hills, where the Bannock Burn rises [*Watson (1926), 195-6*]. Maen Gwyngwn was therefore a place in Pictland. So do these references prove conclusively that the Picts were Britons like the men of Gododdin? No, but they do seem to suggest that by AD 600 there were people of Brittonic descent and sympathies living "north of the border".

32   Pennar, M, *Taliesin Poems* (Llanerch, Felinfach, 1988)
33   Jackson, K H, *The Gododdin: The Oldest Scottish Poem* (Edinburgh Univ Press, Edinburgh, 1969)

Adamnan (c AD 680)[34]

The Life of Saint Columba I 7
"On the Battle of the Miathi"
[*there follows an account of how Columba prophesied the outcome of a battle between the Scots under King Aidan, and the Miathi*]

I, 8
[*Columba prophecies which of Aidan's sons will succeed him*]
For Artur and Eochoid Find were not long afterward killed in the above-mentioned battle of the Miathi...

I, 29
But another story concerning the great and wonderful power of his voice should not be omitted. The fact is said to have taken place near the fortress of King Brude (near Inverness).

II, 10
Again, while the blessed man was stopping for some days in the province of the Picts, he heard that there was a fountain famous among this heathen people, which foolish men, having their senses blinded by the devil, worshipped as a god. [*There follows an account of how Columba exorcised the demon.*]

II, 33
At the time when St Columba was tarrying for some days in the province of the Picts, a certain peasant who, with his whole family, had listened to and learned through an interpreter the word of life preached by the holy man, believed and was baptised — the husband, together with his wife, children and domestics.

II, 34
[*On the exchange of spells with a Pictish Druid named Broichan*]
About the same time, the venerable man, from motives of humanity, besought Broichan the Druid to liberate a certain Scotic female slave, and when he cruelly and

34 Reeves, W, *Adamnan - Life of Saint Columba* (Historians of Scotland, Edmonston, 1874)

73

obstinately refused to part with her, the saint then spoke to him to the following effect: "Know, O Broichan, and be assured that if thou refuse to set this captive free, as I desire thee, that thou shalt die suddenly before I take my departure again from this province". Having said this in the presence of Brude, the king, he departed from the royal palace and proceeded to the river Nesa;...[*there follows an account of the blessing of a pebble from the Ness, which was then used to free Broichan from the spell. In II 35 Broichan summons up a storm to delay the departure of Columba's boat.*]

II, 43
[*On the departure of the adventurer Cormac upon a voyage of exploration*]
After he had gone far from the land over the boundless ocean at full sail, St Columba, who was then staying beyond the Dorsal Ridge of Britain (Drumalban), recommended him in the following terms to King Brude, in the presence of the ruler of the Orcades...

II, 47
...Scotia (Ireland) and Britain have twice been ravaged by a dreadful pestilence throughout the whole of their length, except among the two tribes, the Picts and Scots of Britain, who are separated from each other by the dorsal mountains of Britain.

Brude is the first name in the Pictish king-lists who can be historically verified and his reign therefore marks the terminal point of the present study. In the sixth century, Brude appears to be king only of the northern Picts, with a separate, or sub-ruler of the Orkneys; and with the southern Miathi (Maeatae) retaining a degree of independence. The west coast had already been lost to the Scots.

The Anonymous Life of Saint Cuthbert (c AD 699-705)[35]

IV
At another time also, he went from the same monastery which is called Melrose with two brothers, and, setting

35   Colgrave, B, *Two Lives of St Cuthbert* (Cambridge 1940)

sail for the land of the Picts, they reached the land called the region of the Niuduera in safety.

Bede (c AD 721)[36]

The Life of Saint Cuthbert XI
Now at a certain time, having left the monastery on account of some necessity which arose, he came by boat to the land of the Picts who are called Niduari, accompanied by two brethren, one of whom afterwards became a priest.

The anonymous life, which was Bede's main source refers to *Niuduera regio*, but Bede does not say that it was a region. Colgrave's edition of 1940 gives other manuscript variants, such as *Niudwera*, *Niduuari*, and *Niudpaeralegio*; and suggests that the original form must have been *Nuid-*. I have not pursued here the connection with the so-called Picts of Galloway mentioned in other twelfth century English sources.

Bede (AD 731)[37]

Ecclesiastical History 1, 1
At the present time there are in Britain, in harmony with the five books of the divine law, five languages and four nations — English, British, Scots and Picts. Each of these have their own language; but all are united in their study of God's truth by the fifth — Latin — which has become a common medium through the study of the scriptures. At first the only inhabitants of the island were the Britons, from whom it takes its name, and who, according to tradition, crossed into Britain from Armorica [Brittany] and occupied the southern parts. When they had spread northwards and occupied the greater part of the island, it is said that some Picts from Scythia put to sea in a few longships and were driven by storms around the coasts of Britain, arriving at length on the north coast of Ireland. Here they found the nation of the Scots, from whom they

36 Colgrave, B, *Two Lives of St Cuthbert* (Cambridge 1940)
37 Sherley-Price, L, *Bede - A History of the English Church and People* (Penguin, Harmondsworth, 1968)

asked permission to settle; but their request was refused. Ireland is the largest island after Britain and lies to the west of it. It is shorter than Britain to the north, but extends beyond it to the south towards the northern coasts of Spain, although a wide sea separates them. These Pictish seafarers, as I have said, asked for a grant of land so that they too could make a settlement. The Scots replied that there was not room for them both, but said: "We can give you good advice. We know that there is another island not far to the east, which we often see in the distance on clear days. If you choose to go there, you can make it fit to live in; should you meet resistance, we will come to your help". So the Picts crossed into Britain, and began to settle in the north of the island, since the Britons were in possession of the south. Having no women with them, these Picts asked wives of the Scots, who consented on condition that when any dispute arose, they should choose a king from the female royal line rather than the male. This custom continues among the Picts to this day. As time went on, Britain received a third nation, that of the Scots, who migrated from Ireland under their chief Reuda and by a combination of force and treaty, obtained from the Picts the settlements that they still hold. From the name of this chieftain they are still known as Dealreudians, for in their tongue *dal* means a division.

1, 5
[*On the building of the northern wall*]
He [*Severus*] was compelled to come to Britain by the desertion of nearly all the tribes allied to Rome, and after many critical and hard-fought battles he decided to separate that portion of the island under his control from the remaining unconquered peoples.

Although Bede's account is written five hundred years after the events, he seems to imply here that the northern tribes had previously been allies of Rome. However, this cannot be confirmed from the more contemporary information of either Dio Cassius or Herodian. It seems to have originated from Eutropius (Against the Pagans, VII,17,7).

1, 12

[On the rebuilding of the northern wall]

...Consequently for many years this region suffered attacks from two savage extraneous races, Scots from the north-west and Picts from the north. I term these races extraneous, not because they came from outside Britain, but because their lands were sundered from that of the Britons: for two estuaries lay between...

...Clear traces of this wide and lofty earthwork can be seen to this day. It begins about two miles west of the monastery of Aebbercurnig at a place which the Picts call *Peanfahel* and the English Penneltun and runs westward to the vicinity of the city of Alcluith. But as soon as their old enemies saw...

III, 3

[On the monastery at Iona]

...The island itself belongs to Britain and is separated from the mainland only by a narrow strait; but the Picts living in that part of Britain gave it to the Scots monks long ago, because they received the faith of Christ through their preaching.

III, 4

[On the conversion of the northern Picts by Columba]

In the year of our lord 565, when Justin the Younger succeeded Justinian as Emperor of Rome, a priest and abbot named Columba, distinguished by his monastic habit and life, came from Ireland to Britain to preach the word of God in the provinces of the northern Picts, which are separated from those of the southern Picts by a range of steep and desolate mountains.

The southern Picts, who live this side of the mountains, are said to have abandoned the errors of idolatry long before this date and accepted the true Faith through the preaching of the Bishop Ninian, a most reverend and holy man of British race...

...Columba arrived in Britain in the ninth year of the reign of the powerful Pictish king Bridei mac Maelchon...

I have omitted here Bede's discussion of the Pictish errors in the calculation of Easter and Abbot Coelfrid's letter to the Pictish King Nechtan on these matters (c AD 710).

Nennius (c 830 AD)[38]

Historia Brittonum, 12

After an interval of many years, not less than 800, Picts came and occupied the islands called Orkney, and later from the islands they wasted many lands, and occupied those in the northern part of Britain, and they still live there today. They held and hold a third part of Britain to this day.

15

...But the Scots who are in the west, and the Picts from the north, fought together in a united assault on the British unremittingly...

21

After him [*Julius*] the second emperor to come was Claudius, and he ruled in Britain 48 years after the coming of Christ, and fought a great and bloody battle, not without loss to his troops, but however he was victorious in Britain. Afterwards, he went with his keels to the Orkney Islands and conquered them and made them tributary.

23

Severus was the third to cross to the British. To protect the subject provinces from barbarian invasion, he built a wall rampart there, which is called Guaul in the British language...that is 132 miles from Penguaul, a place which is called Cenail in Irish, Peneltun in English, to the estuary of the Clyde and Caer Pentaloch, where it finishes. The said Severus built it ruggedly, but in vain. The emperor Carausius rebuilt it later, and fortified it with seven forts, between the two estuaries, and a Round House of polished stone, on the banks of the river Carron, which takes its name from him; he erected a triumphal arch to commemorate his victory. Severus ordered the wall to be built between the British and Picts and Irish, because the Irish from the west and the Picts from the north were fighting against the British, for they were at peace with each other...

38 Morris, J, *Nennius, British History and the Welsh Annals* (Phillimore, London, 1980)

30

The Roman generals were killed by the British on three occasions. But when the British were harassed by the barbarian nations, that is the Irish and the Picts, they implored the Romans to help...

38

[*In the context of the Fifth Century settlement of Vortigern's English mercenaries*]
...They sailed around the Picts and wasted the Orkney Islands and came and occupied many districts beyond the Frenessican Sea, as far as the borders of the Picts.

Cormac's Glossary (tenth century)[39]

301 Catit or Cartait : Cruthnian language: a thorn or pin

The Pictish Chronicle or Chronicle of the Kings (tenth century)[40]

[*These extracts are translated from the text of the introduction in Skene's "Chronicles" The pre-historical part of the king list has been summarised in Appendix D.*]

The Picts, in their own language, are named from their painted bodies, perhaps a comment because they brand themselves with various figures using ink and an iron needle. The Scots, who now are corruptly called Irish, rather are Sciti from the Scythian Region, because they have originally derived from there; or perhaps from Scotta a daughter of a royal pharaoh of Egypt...the Britons came to Britain in the third age of the world; but the Scitae, that is to say the Scots, came to Scotland in the fourth age; and to Ireland, where they prevail. The Scythians are white haired; they are born with hair and skin as white as snow and from this are named Albani: from them have derived both the Scots and the Picts...[*There follows a lengthy discussion of the Goths and Scythians; and then the king list*]

39   Meyer, K, *Sanas Cormaic* (Dublin, 1913, reprinted by Llanerch, Felinfach, 1994)
40   Skene, W F, *Chronicles of the Picts, Chronicles of the Scots, and other early Memorials of Scottish History* (Edinburgh, 1867)

This introduction, as Innes pointed out, is copied almost word-for-word from the *Origines* of Isidore of Seville (references: IX ii 103; IX ii 65; IX ii 27; XIV iii 31; XIV iv 3; XI ii 65). Its author has substituted "Picts" for "Scots" in the first sentence and inserted the legend about Scotta, the Egyptian princess (which comes from Nennius); and also the remark that both the Picts and the Scots trace their origin from this same migration. The rest of the introduction can be traced all the way back, via Isidore, to ultimate sources in Solinus, Pliny and Herodotus.

The Annals of Tigernach (eleventh century)[41]

[*While Marcus Antoninus ruled in Rome c AD 172*]
The kingship (was taken) by men of Munster every second time until Conn of the Hundred Battles, for seven kings of the Picts [*Chruithnechaib*] had ruled Ireland.

[*While Maximinus was emperor in Rome c AD 238*]
A battle at Fothaird Muirthemne, in which Cormac, a grandson of Conn, and Fiacha Broad Crown, king of Munster, routed the Picts [*Cruthniu*] and Fiacha Araide, ubi etc.

Whitley Stokes translated Cruithni as "Picts" here, as he does for later entries that clearly relate to the Picts of Scotland.

Irish and Pictish Additions to the Historia Brittonum (before 1072)[42]

[*The following extracts are taken from the translations made by William Skene from the Irish manuscripts. Several manuscript variants of various ages exist (labelled A to G by Skene) and he suggests that the versions in the Book of Ballimote and the Book of Lecain (A and B) preserve the original Irish translation of Nennius by Gilcaemhin. Skene thought that these preserved the oldest form of the Pictish settlement tradition; as the text states that it was taken from the books of the Cruthneach. The reader is referred to Skene for the full texts. These selected extracts are only intended to illustrate those traditions of origin that may have been current among the Picts themselves.*]

41 Stokes, W *The Annals of Tigernach* (reprinted from *Revue Celtique* 1895/96, Llanerch, Felinfach, 1993)
42 Skene, W F, *Chronicles of the Picts, Chronicles of the Scots, and other early Memorials of Scottish History* (Edinburgh, 1867)

Afterwards came a company of eight, with a fleet, and dwelt in Erin, and took possession of a great portion of it.

The Firbolg, moreover, took possession of Manand, and certain islands in like manner, Ara, Isla and Recca.

The children of Gleoin, son of Ercol, took possession of the islands of Orcc, that is, Historend, son of Historrim, sone of Agam, son of Agathirsi, and were dispersed again from the islands of Orcc; that is Cruthne, son of Cinge, son of Luctai, son of Parthai, son of Historech, went and took possession of the north of the island of Britain, and his seven sons divided the land into seven divisions; and Onbecan, son of Caith, son of Cruthne took the sovereignty of the seven divisions.

Finach was lord of Erin at that time, and took hostages of the Cruthneach.

Five of the Cruthneach of the island of Orc, moreover, viz., five brothers of the father of the Cruthneach, went to France and founded a city there, viz, Pictavis its name, and came again to the island, that is, to Erin, where they were for a long time, till the Gael drove them across the sea to their brethren.

Of the Origin of the Cruthneach here:

Cruithne, son of Cinge, son of Luctai, son of Partalan, son of Agnoin, son of Buain, son of Mais, son of Fathecht, son of Jafeth, son of Noe.

He was the father of the Cruthneach, and reigned a hundred years.

These are the seven sons of Cruthne, viz, Fib, Fidach, Fodla, Fortrend, warlike, Cait, Ce, Cirig; and they divided the land into seven divisions, as Columcille says:

Seven children of Cruithne
Divided Alban into seven divisions.
Cait, Ce, Cirig, a warlike clan,
Fib, Fidach, Fotla, Fortrenn.

And the name of each man is given to the territories, as Fib, Ce, Cait, and the rest.

Thirteen kings of them took possession.

Fib reigned twenty-four years.

Fidhach, forty years.
Fortrenn, seventy.
Cait, twenty-two years.
Ce, twelve years.
Cirig, eight years.
Aenbecan, son of Cait, thirty years.
Finechta, sixty years.
Guidid gadbre, that is geis, one year.
Gest gurid, forty.
Urges, thirty years.

Brude Pont, thirty kings of them, and Bruide was the name of each man of them, and of the divisions of the other men. They possessed an hundred and fifty years, as it is in the books of the Cruthneach.

Brude pont.
Brude urpont.
Brude leo.
Brude uleo.
Brude gant.
Brude urgant.
Brude gnith.
Brude urgnith.
Brude feth.
Brude urfeichir.
Brude cal.
Brude urcal.
Brude cint.
Brude urcint.
Brude feth.
Brude urfeth.
Brude ru.
Brude ero.
Brude gart.
Brude urgart.
Brude cind.
Brude urcind.
Brude uip.
Brude uruip.
Brude grith.
Brude urgrith.
Brude muin.
Brude urmuin.

C

And Alban was without a king all that time, till the period of Gud, the first king who possessed all Alban by consent or by force. Others say that it was Cathluan, son of Caitmind, who possessed the kingdom by force in Cruthintuath and in Erin for sixty years, and that after him Gud possessed fifty years. [*There follows the list of kings up to the historical period*]

D

The Cruthneach came from the land of Thracia; that is they are the children of Gleoin, son of Ercol. Agathirsi was their name. Six brothers of them came at first, viz, Solen, Ulfa, Nechtan, Drostan, Aengus, Leithenn. The cause of their coming: Policornus king of Thrace fell in love with their sister, and proposed to take her without a dower. They after this passed over Roman territory into France, and built a city there, viz , Pictavis, *a Pictis*, that is, from their arms...
[*there follows an account of the voyage of the Cruthneach to Ireland and thereafter to Britain in explanation of the origin of the Picts in both countries. The origin of their name "Pict" is explained in verse.*]

Thracia was the name of their country,
Till they spread their sails,
After they had resolved to emigrate,
In the east of Europe.

Agathyrsi was their name
In the portion of Erchbi
From their tattooing their fair skins
Were they called Picti.

It is difficult to add much to Skene's conclusion that the Cruithni are "taken in their wanderings to every part of Europe where the name of Picti or Pictones could be found, and connected to every people who resembled them, either in name or of whom the custom of painting the body, by puncturing the skin, which was their characteristic, is recorded". It can only be the present author's assessment, but it seems that we see here the muddling of two separate traditions: one being the origin of a group of Britons, from Gaul: the other a similar-sounding tale about the origin of the northern Picts, at some late period after the two groups had merged; this has then been prefixed to the list of Pictish kings. The existence of two separate traditions of origin is reliably recorded by Bede. The Roman sources tell us that all the Britons painted their bodies with blue woad, but that only some of them (the true Picts) tattooed their faces and bodies with designs; this may have been the root of the confusion.

In Skene's translation the sojourn of the Cruithni in Ireland is described, together with an account of their taking of Irish wives and the swearing of an oath that succession should be via the female line. Their migration to northern Britain is then related.

> They passed away from us,
> With the splendour of swiftness,
> To dwell by valour
> In the land of the country beyond Ile.

> From thence they conquered Alba
> The noble nurse of fruitfulness.
> Without destroying the people
> From the region of Cat to Forchu.
> ...

E

Cruithnechan, the son of Lochit, son of Ingi, went over from the sons of Mileadh to the Britons of Fortrenn to fight against the Saxons; and he defended the country of Cruithentuaith for them, and he himself remained with them. But they had no women, for the women of Alba had died. And Cruithnechan went back to the sons of Mileadh, and he swore...that the regal succession among them for ever should be on the mother's side; and he took away with him twelve women that were superabundant with the sons of Mileadh, for their husbands had been drowned in the western sea along with Donn; so that the chiefs of the Cruithneach have been of the men of Erin from that time ever since.

The reference here to Saxons would suggest that the origins of the legend of the taking of Irish wives is post-Roman and has become confused with older material. The name of the Cruithneach is here seen to be associated with the "Britons" of Fortrenn [*Breatnu Foirtren*].

De Situ Albanie (after 1165)[43]

[*This extract is taken from Skene's "Chronicles" and enables the seven Pictish provinces to be identified.*]

Now this land was divided anciently by seven brothers into seven parts. Of these the principal is Angus with Mearns, so named after Oengus, the eldest of the brothers. And the second is Athole and Gowrie. The third part is Strathearn with Monteith. The fourth of the parts is Fife with Fothreff; and the fifth part is Mar, with Buchan. The sixth is Moray and Ross. The seventh part is Caithness, to this side of the mountain, and beyond the mountain; because the mountain of Mound divides Caithness through the middle.

Ailred of Rievaulx, (twelfth century)[44]

The Life of Saint Ninian, VI
He undertaketh the Conversion of the Picts — He returneth home...
...he invaded the empire of the strong man [*i.e. The Devil*] armed, with the purpose of rescuing from his power innumerable victims of his captivity: wherefore, attacking the Southern Picts, whom still the Gentile error which clung to them induced to reverence and worship deaf and dumb idols...

Ninian worked from Whithorn in Galloway during the second quarter of the Fifth century; and according to Bede it was he who first converted the southern Picts. The oldest source for Ninian's life is an eighth century poem *Miracula Nynie Episcopi* which drew upon the same source as Ailred: a lost book written in a "barbarous" style of Latin. Here the southern Picts are named *Naturae*, which has been convincingly explained as a scribal error for the *Niduari* mentioned in the Life of St Cuthbert. On this connection see W Levinson (1940).

43   Skene, W F, *Chronicles of the Picts, Chronicles of the Scots, and other early Memorials of Scottish History* (Edinburgh, 1867)
44   Forbes, A P (ed), *Lives of St Ninian and St Kentigern* (Historians of Scotland, Edinburgh 1874)

Joceline (late twelfth century)[45]

The Life of Saint Kentigern, XXXIV

...after he had converted what was nearest to himself, that is to say, his diocese, going forth to more distant places, cleansed from the foulness of idolatry and the contagion of heresy the land of the Picts, which is now called Galwiethia, with adjacent parts...

For he went to Albania, and there with great and almost unbearable toil, often exposed to death by the snares of the barbarians...he reclaimed that land from the worship of idols and from profane rites that were almost equal to idolatry...

Any discussion as to the existence of Picts in Galloway during historical times must lie beyond the scope of a study of Pictish origins. Galloway is a name of later origin and on Ptolemy's map the peninsula is occupied by the Novantae ("new-tribe"). Of more importance here is to note that that an outlying group of brochs is found there, which may indicate settlement from the north during earlier times. Further ambiguity arises as to whether these, rather than the Maeatae, were the so-called "southern Picts" converted by Ninian; and hence whether Galloway was the Niuduera region.

Historia Norwegiae (twelfth century)[46]

Of the Orchades Islands.

These islands were first inhabited by the Picts and Papae [*Irish monks*]. Of these the one race, the Picts, little exceeded pigmies in stature; they did marvels, in the morning and in the evening, in building [walled] towns, but at mid-day they entirely lost all their strength, and lurked, through fear, in little underground houses. But at that time [the islands] were not called Orchades, but Pictland; whence still the Pictland Sea is named by the inhabitants, because it divides the islands from Scotland...Whence the people came there, we are entirely ignorant...

45 Forbes, A P (ed), *Lives of St Ninian and St Kentigern* (Historians of Scotland, Edinburgh 1874)
46 Anderson, A O, *Early Sources of Scottish History, AD 500-1286, Volume 1* (Oliver & Boyd, Edinburgh 1922)

In the days of Harold Fairhair, king of Norway, certain pirates of the family of the most vigorous prince Ronald, set out with a great fleet, and crossed the Solundic sea; and stripped these races of their ancient settlements, destroyed them wholly, and subdued the islands to themselves.

Here the Picts are called *Peti* and their country *Terra Petorum;* and *Petlandicum Mare* is the Pentland Firth. The Norse conquest is datable to 874 and therefore lies beyond the scope of this study. It has been suggested that *Peti* may be the original form of the name Pict, rather than a derivation from Latin *pictus*. The Picts are seen to be associated with the brochs even at this late date and the thoroughness of the conquest explains the almost total replacement of Pictish place names by Norse names throughout Caithness and the northern isles.

Geoffrey of Monmouth (1136)[47]

The History of the Kings of Britain, i, 2
Lastly, Britain is inhabited by five races of people, the Norman-French, the Britons, the Saxons, the Picts and the Scots. Of these, the Britons once occupied the land from sea to sea before the others came. Then the vengeance of God overtook them because of their arrogance and they submitted to the Picts and the Saxons...

iv, 14
...With the help of Arvirargus he [*Claudius*] subdued the Orkneys and the other islands in that neighbourhood.

iv, 17
Marius, the son of Arvirargus, succeeded him in the kingship. He was a man of peace and wisdom. A little later on in his reign a certain King of the Picts called Sodric came from Scythia with a large fleet and landed in the northern part of Britain which is called Albany. He began to ravage Marius's lands. Marius therefore collected his men together and marched to meet Sodric...

47 Thorpe, L, *Geoffrey of Monmouth: The History of the Kings of Britain* (Penguin, Harmondsworth, 1966 [repr 1987])

...Once Sodric was killed and the people who had come with him were beaten, Marius gave them the part of Albany called Caithness to live in. The land had been desert and untilled for many a long day, for no-one lived there. Since they had no wives, the Picts asked the Britons for their daughters and kinswomen; but the Britons refused to marry off their womenfolk to such manner of men. Having suffered this rebuff, the Picts crossed over to Ireland and married women from that country. Children were born to these women and in this way the Picts increased their numbers. This is enough about them, for it is not my purpose to describe Pictish history, nor indeed that of the Scots, who trace their descent from them, and from the Irish, too.

v, 2

When Sulgenius was no longer able to resist Severus, he crossed the sea to Scythia, hoping to be restored to power with the help of the Picts. He collected together all the young men of that country, returned to Britain with a huge fleet and besieged York.

It is impossible to treat Geoffrey as a source of history. His account of a Pictish settlement from Scythia elaborates on that of Bede and others. The curious synchronisms of Geoffrey would place the invasion of Sodric and his Picts in the reign of the Emperor Vespasian; and the campaign of Sulgenius appears to correlate with the revolt of the Maeatae. These events are not entirely implausible and should not be dismissed out of hand. Geoffrey's History was subsequently translated from Latin into Welsh and these versions are colloquially known as the Welsh "Bruts", although some of the Welsh versions may even predate the History. All that need be said here is that they introduce the confusion of Geoffrey's Welsh-derived mythology into the older traditions of Pictish origins. Skene listed a number of variants and derivatives from the Bruts, however I shall not pursue them further here.

The Annals of Clonmacnoise (after 1408)[48]

[Extracts from the English translation made in 1627 by Conell Mageoghan from an Irish manuscript now lost.]

> *[At some time before the birth of Christ and while the Milesians ruled in Ireland, three of the royal brothers and some 100 sailors have been drowned in storms at sea.]*
> They alsoe say that the picts heareing of ye great number of widowes in Ireland, came & married the relict widows of the said drowned persons & covenanted with the sons of Miletus that if they had failed Issue male, y^t then the ofspring of Miletus should inherit theire Contry, which accordingly came to pass after a long space, for in Defect of their Issue one fergus, the king of Ireland's son was sent over into Scotland & was Invested as King thereof; they were called Picts of a certain oyntment they used to paint theire faces wth all; their land in English is called pictland, in Irish *criocha cruitneach.*

Here we see another confusion in the naming of the Picts from the widespread British custom of body painting, rather than from their tattooing (compare: Isidore).

> ...The Picts made great warrs wth the Brittaines...[*There follows an account of how the Picts fled when the Britons under Germanus and Lupus sang loudly Alleluia.*]

These events are dated to 429 by the life of Saint Germanus.

> 449...Drust m^{c}Erb, K of Pictland Died...

Morris's comparison of all the Irish annals revises the death of Drust to about AD 454, but his reign still cannot be regarded as historically confirmed.

> ...The Scottish men were put to flight by Brwydy m^{c}Milcon K of Picts...the sayleing of St Columb Kill to Scotland in the 42nd yeare of his age.

48   Murphy, Rev D (ed), *The Annals of Clonmacnoise* (Univ of Dublin, 1896)

580...Ceannath K of the Picts dyed.

564 - Brwydy m^cMilcon, K of Pictland dyed...

The accepted date for Brude's death is 584. Although Brude is king throughout this period, Adamnan's life of Columba also indicates a sub-ruler of the Orkneys; and an independent kingdom of the Miathi or southern Picts at this era.

The Welsh Triads (of uncertain era)[48]

From the Triads of Arthur, 36
Three Oppressions that came to this island, and not one of them went back:
One of them (was) the people of the Corianiaid, who came here in the time of Caswallawn son of Beli: and not one of them went back. And they came from Arabia.
The second Oppression: the Gwyddyl Ffichti. And not one of them went back.
The third Oppression: the Saxons, with Horsa and Hengist as their leaders.

The triads of Arthur are generally treated as authentic. The name *Gvydyl Fychti* for the Picts first occurs in the Welsh Bruts, but may be older. In the *Third Series Triads* are also found the triad of the Three Refugee Tribes and the triad of the Three Predatory Hordes; the latter seemingly an expansion of the above. These triads were quoted by Skene, but have long been condemned as likely forgeries. The Celyddon (Caledonians) and Gwyddyl (Scots/Irish) are separately listed among the refugee tribes (i.e. they were given permission to settle), whereas the Gwyddyl Ffichti are given as predatory invaders who came across the North Sea.

49   Bromwich, R, *Troiedd Ynys Prydein* (Cardiff 1961 [repr 1978])

Appendices

Appendix A

A "Scythian" Homeland for the Picts?

According to the various traditions, the Picts descended from a colony of "Scythian" or "Thracian" seafarers who took wives from among the Irish before settling in the Orkney Islands and northern Scotland. The only reliable authority to offer this account is Bede and he could have learned it from the Irish sources. W J Watson, [*1926, pp 60-61*] convincingly dismissed the legends as merely "learned Irish" embellishment, based on the mention of "picti Agathyrsi" and "picti Geloni" in the Aeneid of Virgil. This, together with the account by Herodotus that traces the descent of these nations from the three sons of Heracles: Agathyrsus, Gelonus and Scythes, led the Irish to divert the Picts" point of origin from Scythia to Thrace. Watson believed the less elaborate accounts offered by Gildas and Nennius to be more reliable.

Herodotus, writing at about 450 BC, locates the Agathyrsi on the Black Sea above the Danube, and the Geloni, he says, were Greeks who settled in the territory of the Budini on the upper Dnieper. All these tribes were, at that era, tributary to the Scythians. Herodotus also describes the social organisation of the Agathyrsi: they held their women in common and were all therefore brothers, as of a single family. This is remarkably similar to the customs attributed to British tribes by Julius Caesar, Dio Cassius, Solinus and St Jerome. The free social customs of the Miathi and the matrilineal succession of the Picts would certainly have been known to the educated Irish and it is plausible that they made the connection.

Before we discard these legends as mere invention by the learned Irish perhaps we should again take note of Solinus, who records that the Agathyrsi dyed their hair and faces blue, just as we are told that the Britons did. Both Britons and the Albani of Scythia are said to have bred fierce dogs; and as we shall see, similar forms of cannibalism appear to have been practised both in Ireland and throughout Scythia. These similarities exist in the sources and may not be simply glossed over as an invention of the Irish monks. Indeed the earliest tradition of "Greeks" migrating to Britain in the train of Heracles must be at least as old as that given in Plutarch's essay, *The Face in the Moon* (first century AD).

Neither was the practice of tattooing and body painting restricted to the British Isles. The tattooing of animal figures onto the skin was apparently a widespread custom throughout the Scythian region, as such depictions have recently been found on the body of a Scythian chieftain excavated at Pazyryk, in the Altai region of Russia [*Brothwell 1976, pl 4*]. Similar animals have been found depicted on artefacts from Scythian tombs [*Rudenko, 1970 109-14*]. Therefore there is no necessity, as some writers do, to derive the British customs of body decoration as a custom that the "Celts" adopted in the east through contact with Scythian tribes; when indigenous traditions plainly tell us that their practitioners were themselves a race of "Scythian" origin.

However, any suggestion that the Picts came from "Scythia" must be placed on a firmer foundation than Irish legends. If we suppose the various legends to have some basis in truth then the migration must have occurred at some point before the earliest historical mention of the Picts, perhaps before Agricola (AD 84) but certainly before AD 200. The Pictish king lists, taken at face value, would suggest a date as early as 500 BC. We should also be mindful that more than one such migration may have occurred.

Since the Picts were certainly a maritime nation, it follows that we should look for a point of origin somewhere along the Baltic coast, which some early writers referred to as the Scythian Coast. Just as we know that the ancestors of the later Anglo-Saxon invaders are hidden within the Roman descriptions of Germany, so it is possible that the predecessors of the Picts could lie hidden within the early classical ethnography of the Baltic coast. It is worthwhile that we should look at these to see if there are any points of similarity.

The earliest surviving description of the Baltic region is that of Herodotus. It is evident that he knew little of northern Europe beyond the hinterland of the Black Sea trading area of the Greeks, which extended as far up the Dnieper as Kiev. Farther inland the trade was monopolised by the Scythians. Starting from the Danube eastwards, he names nations subject to the Scythians that can be recognised in later reports—and some that cannot: Tauri, Agathyrsi, Neuri, Androphagi, Melanchlaeni, Geloni, Budini, Sauromatae and Issedones, together with semi-mythical Arimaspi and Hyperboreans; the true Scythians were probably Iranians. The following is a selection of the most useful references.

Herodotus (c 450 BC)[1]

Histories III, 113
[*On his ignorance of the northern coast of Europe*]
I have never found anyone who could give me first-hand information of the existence of a sea beyond Europe to the north and west. Yet it cannot be disputed that tin and amber do come to us...

IV, 14
The Scythians extend eastward...and northwards as far up the Borysthenes [*Dneiper*] as a boat can sail in eleven days. Further north is a great tract of uninhabited desert, beyond which live the Androphagi —the maneaters—who have no connection with the Scythians but are a quite distinct race. Northward again, so far as we can tell, there is utter desert without trace of human life.

IV, 27
Some knowledge of the practices of the Issedones has come through to us: for instance when a man's father dies, his kinsmen bring sheep to his house as a sacrificial offering; the sheep and the body of the dead man are cut into joints and sliced up, and the two sorts of meat, mixed together, are served and eaten. The dead man's head, however, they gild, after stripping off the hair and cleaning out the inside, and then preserve it as a sort of sacred image, to which they offer sacrifice...

1   De Selincourt, A, *Herodotus: The Histories* (Penguin, Harmondsworth 1954 [repr 1988])

In other respects the Issedones have a sound enough
sense of the difference between right and wrong, and a
remarkable thing about them is that men and women
have equal authority...

This description of the equal authority of the sexes among
the Issedones is a strong indicator that they were Finno-
Ugrians, as this is a characteristic of their customs and
languages.

IV, 105
The Androphagi are the most savage of men, and have
no notion of either law or justice. They are herdsmen
without fixed dwellings; their dress is Scythian, their
language is peculiar to themselves, and they are the
only people in this part of the world to eat human flesh.

Having said that the Androphagi (simply Greek: "man-
eaters") are the only cannibals, he forgets that he has previously
described a cannibalistic practice among the Issedones. The
location of the Androphagi would lie in modern Belarus or the
Baltic States. That these are indeed closely related tribes is
later confirmed by Pomponius Mela, Pliny and Solinus.

Diodorus Siculus (c 50 BC)[2]

Library of History, V, 31, 2-3
[*As an aside within his description of the Gauls*]
The most savage people among them are those who
dwell beneath the Bears and on the borders of Scythia,
and some of these, we are told, eat human beings, even
as the Britons do who dwell on the island of Iris...

I did not include this with the Pictish sources since it refers
to Britons living in Ireland. This may well be a reference to the
Cruithni of Ireland — since it is generally agreed that that
name is an Irish form of *Priteni* "Britons". The Gauls [*Galatoi*]
"living beneath the Bears" (i.e. the northern constellations)
could refer to north Britain. Diodorus did not distinguish the
Germans from the Celts, so his cannibalistic Gauls "on the
borders of the Scythians" may therefore imply the Androphagi
or the Issedones. Despite their undoubted barbarity, there is

2   Oldfather, C H, *Diodorus Siculus*, Vol 3 (Harvard University Press, Cambridge,
Massachusets 1993)

no report of any cannibalistic practices among the Picts of Britain, unless we allow St Jerome's report of the Attacotti.

Strabo (c 7 BC)[3]

Geography II, 5, 7
Above the Borysthenes dwell Roxolani, the most remote of the known Scythians, though they are further south than the furthest known people of the British Isles; the regions beyond are already uninhabitable, because of the cold. Further south are the Sauromatae. [*Sarmatians*]

IV, 5, 4
Besides some small islands round Britain there is also a large island, Ierne [*Ireland*]... Concerning this island I have nothing to tell, except that its inhabitants are more savage than the Britons, since they are man-eaters as well as heavy eaters, and since further, they count it an honourable thing, when their fathers die, to devour them, and openly to have intercourse, not only with other women, but also with their mothers and sisters; but I am saying this only with the understanding that I have no trustworthy witness for it; and yet, as for the matter of man-eating, that is said to be a custom of the Scythians also...[*Strabo continues that Celts and Iberians have only practised cannibalism when besieged.*]

Strabo is clearly referring here to the same Irish "cannibalism" as Diodorus above; and in likening it to a Scythian custom his description of them must be equated with that of the Issedones previously described by Herodotus. The free sexual practices are similar to those described elsewhere of northern British tribes; and also of the Scots. Therefore we need not doubt that the race referred to here are the Cruithni of Ireland.

3   Jones, H L, *The Geography of Strabo* (Harvard University Press, Cambridge, Massachusets, 1988)

Pomponius Mela (c AD 40)[4]

[Translated from the text of P Parroni]

De Choreographica II, 8-10
The Essedones celebrate their deceased parents joyfully, drawing together their household to offer rites of sacrifice. The flesh itself they butcher and blend with the meat of other beasts, which they distribute to their guests to consume. The skull, they skilfully polish and adorn with gold...

Pliny (c AD 40)[5]

Natural History IV, xii, 81
[*The extent of Scythia*]
The name of the Scythians has spread in every direction, as far as the Sarmatae and the Germans, but this old designation has not continued in use for any except the most outlying sections of these races...

By the first century AD the Sarmatians had expanded westward into the former Scythian hegemony. Pliny is using old sources.

IV xii, 88
[*His description of the interior of Northern Scythia*]
... The interior of the mainland is occupied by the Auchetai and the Neuroi, in whose territories respectively are the sources of the Bug and the Dneiper, the Geloni, Thyssagatae, Budini, Basilidae and Agathyrsi, the last a dark-haired people; above them are the nomads and cannibals [*Anthropophagi*], and after Lake Buces above the Sea of Azov the Sauromatae and Essedones.

IV, xiii, 94-5
[*Part of his description of The "Scythian" Coast*]
... In this direction a number of islands are reported to exist that have no names, but according to the account of Timaeus there is one named Baunonia, lying off

4   Parroni, P, *Pomponii Melae* (De Chorographia, Rome, 1984)
5   Rackham, H, *Pliny - Natural History*, Vol 2 (Harvard University Press, Cambridge, Massachusets, 1989)

Scythia, at a distance of a days voyage from the coast, on the beach of which in spring time amber is cast up by the waves. The rest of these coasts are only known by reports of doubtful authority...

IV, xiii, 97
... Some authorities report that these regions as far as the river Vistula are inhabited by the Sarmati, Venedi, Sciri and Hirri [*there follows another account of the collection of amber, again establishing this as the Baltic coast.*]

VII, i, 8-12
We have pointed out that some Scythian tribes, and in fact a good many, feed on human bodies... According to Isogonus of Nicea the former cannibal tribes whom we stated to exist to the north, ten days' journey beyond the river Dneiper, drink out of human skulls and use the scalps with hair on as napkins hung around their necks. The same authority states that certain people in Albania [*here the shores of the Caspian Sea*] are born with keen grey eyes and are bald from childhood, and that they see better by night than by day.

These remarks on cannibalism are further elucidated by reference to Solinus, below.

Tacitus (AD 98)[6]

Germania 38
[*On the customs of the Suebian Germans*]
They occupy more than half of Germany, and are divided into a number of separate tribes under different names, though all are called by the generic title of "Suebi". It is a special characteristic of this nation to comb the hair sideways and tie it in a knot. This distinguishes the Suebi from the rest of the Germans, and among the Suebi, distinguishes the freedman from the slave. Individual men of other tribes adopt the same fashion ... the hair is twisted back so that it stands

6   Mattingley, H, *Tacitus - the Agricola and the Germania* (Penguin, Harmondsworth, 1989)

erect, and is often knotted on the very crown of the
head. The chiefs use an even more elaborate style...

Tacitus goes on to say that the purpose of the Suebian knot
was originally to add height and to make their warriors appear
more terrifying in battle.

43

[*Part of his description of the Suebian tribes who lived
east of the Elbe and Danube*] ... Close behind the
Marcomani and Quadi are the Marsigni, Cotini, Osi,
and Buri. Of these the Marsigni and Buri are exactly
like the Suebi in language and mode of life. The Cotini
and the Osi are not Germans: that is proved by their
languages, Celtic in one case, Pannonian in the other
...

The Marcomani lived in Bohemia, but I have included this
passage because it clearly illustrates that Tacitus could identify
Celts and Celtic languages. He next describes the Lugii,
Gothones and Suiones [*Swedes*] who live "right out in the sea".

45

Beyond the Suiones we find another sea, sluggish and
almost stagnant ...Turning therefore, to the right shore
of the Suebian sea we find it washing the country of
the Aestii, who have the same customs and fashions
as the Suebi, but a language more like the British. They
worship the mother of the gods, and wear, as an
emblem of this cult, the device of a boar, which stands
them instead of armour or human protection ...[*there
follows an account of the growing of wheat and the
collection of amber from the beaches by the Aestii*]

The Aestii are politically part of the Germanic Suebi and
have similar customs, but they are not Germans. Their language
is like that of the Britons, but he does not say that they are
Celts. They lived on the amber producing coast: implying
modern east Prussia and the Baltic States where today we find
Finnic and Baltic speakers. The Aestii are clearly the Estonians
and may be equated with the Essedones of Pliny and the
Issedones of Herodotus; or perhaps part of a unified group of
Baltic Finns under this name, along with their neighbours, the
Fenni. Tacitus says that they carried (*gestare* = to bear or carry)
the form of a wild-pig as emblem of a mother goddess, but is

ambiguous whether this implies that it was tattooed or part of the clothing.

> 46
> Here Suebia ends. I do not know whether to class the tribes of the Peucini, Venedi and Fenni with the Germans or with the Sarmatians ... The Fenni are astonishingly savage and disgustingly poor. They have no proper weapons, no horses, no homes. They eat wild herbs, dress in skins and sleep on the ground ...

The description of the Fenni (the Finnoi of Ptolemy) is similar in both form and location to that of the earlier Androphagi, although the cannibalistic practice is not mentioned. The Fenni are usually assumed to have been the Lapps rather than the Finns. Overall, we need not doubt that there were Finnic-speaking tribes along this part of the Baltic coast.

Solinus (c AD 250)[7]

> Collecteana Rerum Memorabilum 15, 13
> Among the Anthropophags in y part of Asia are numbered the Essedons, who likewise are embewed with the same ungracious fwde. It is the manner of the Essedons to follow the corpes of theyr parents singing: and calling together a knot of their next neighbours, to teare the carkasses a sunder with their teeth, and dressing them with other flesh of beastes to make a feast with them. The skulls of them they bind about with golde, and use them as mazers to drinke in...

Summary and Conclusions

A comparison of the information available about the Picts and their predecessors in Britain and Ireland with that of contemporary nations living on the Baltic coast does yield a number of similarities and coincidences. We have a people living in the Orkney islands and northern Scotland, whose name implies boars or pigs. The Picts tattooed themselves with animal figures, including that of the boar, and also carved them

---

7   Golding A, *Solinus - Collectanea Rerum Memorabilium* (1587, reprinted in facsimile by Scholars Facsimiles and Reprints, Gainsville, Florida, 1955)

on their monuments. We find a Finnic nation on the "Scythian" coast who similarly wore the image of a pig and whose language resembled one spoken in Britain; they also followed similar fashions of hairstyle. Furthermore, we find tribal and place names from the Pictish region that could be of Finnic origin. We then have indigenous traditions that do indeed bring the Picts to Orkney, and to Ireland, as immigrants from Baltic Scythia. The customs of cannibalism, particularly the ritual devouring of the deceased father, are noted from both Scythia and Ireland, and are so unique that it is difficult to see how they could have originated independently.

Appendix B

A Note on the Finno-Ugrian Languages

Studies of the philology of Finno-Ugrian languages, in English for the English reader, are comparatively few. However, for most of the Finnic derivations suggested here, any good dictionary of Finnish or Estonian will suffice to verify them. Two works that have been most useful are *Finno-Ugrian Languages and Peoples* by Peter Hajdu (translated by G Cushing); and *The Structure and Development of the Finnish Language* by Lauri Hakulinen (translated by John Atkinson) The latter identifies the ancient native vocabulary of the Finnic languages and again, most of the roots suggested here are explained.

Linguistic comparisons show that the Finnic languages had split from the Ugrian languages, from which Hungarian descends, well before 1500 BC; and these had further divided from the Permian languages before about 1000 BC The Finnic languages, at some time during the first millennium BC divided again into a Volga group, from which derive Mordvin and Cheremis; and Common or Baltic Finnic, from which derive Finnish, Karelian, Ingrian, Vepsian, Vodian, Estonian and Livonian; but it is generally accepted that Finnish preserves the most archaic forms.

The Finno-Ugrian languages had very early absorbed some Indo-European words from neighbouring languages. The Baltic Finnic peoples were clearly in close contact with Baltic languages (Lithuanian and Old Prussian) up to about AD 500 and also with a Germanic language, probably Gothic; but Slavonic (Russian) loans into Finnish are comparatively recent. Therefore in the context of a postulated migration of Finnic-speaking Picts to Britain at some time between say: 500 BC and 100 AD one might expect to find old Indo-European loans (such as *porsas* "piglet"), some Baltic loans, and possibly some Germanic loans; but no Slavonic words are to be expected.

Hadju comments that by 500 BC the Permians had already split from the Finns and identifies these as the red-haired, blue-eyed, Budini described by Herodotus. The Greeks did not differentiate the Budini from their neighbours, the Geloni. The Issedones of Herodotus are in the right place to be identified with the Volga Finns, while the later Aestii and Fenni would be the western group of Baltic Finns. The name Aestii however, appears to be Germanic, related to English *oast*: "men of the grain drying kilns".

The examination of place or ethnic names requires no great knowledge of Finnic grammar. Finno-Ugrian languages are said to be agglutinative: that is they form new words from simpler components which retain their individual meaning (analogous examples in English might be: house-boat or boat-house) and hence ancient root words tend to be conserved. No native Finnish word ever commences with more than one consonant, or ends with more than two. The consonants *b*, *d*, and *g* occur only in loan words and tend to be replaced by *p*, *t* and *k*; *v* is preferred to *f*. From these simple rules we may deduce that such names as Smertae, Graupius, Brude and Cruithni are unlikely to be of a Finnic origin, whereas others such as Mertae, catait, Orkas, etc., easily could be, even if their meaning is not immediately apparent.

Appendix C

The Brochs of the Maeatae

It has not been the intention here to delve too deeply into archaeological evidence. The difficulty with archaeological papers is that they tend to build upon the preconceived ideas of eminent authorities, without which they would never be accepted for publication in a refereed journal. It is therefore difficult for the non-specialist to go back to source evidence and to dispute long-held conclusions.

A recent synthesis of the archaeological evidence from iron age Caledonia is given by MacKie [*in Green, M J, The Celtic World (1995), pp 654-670*]. Britain north of the Forth and Clyde may be divided into two distinct archaeological provinces: an Atlantic zone north and west of the Highland massif; and a north-eastern province extending from the Forth to the Moray Firth. In the north-east zone are found the remains of the timber laced or "vitrified" forts dating from the eighth century BC, or perhaps earlier. Portable artefacts typical of the continental La Téne Celtic culture occur only in very late deposits from the east coast. Otherwise nothing distinctively "Celtic" is noted from the archaeological finds of iron age Caledonia, either east or west.

The assumption that there *must* have been Celts in this region stems entirely from the supposed presence of the *p*-Celtic Pictish names, for which the usual linguistic authorities are cited. Since the artefacts cannot be positively demonstrated as Celtic, then the concept of a Celtic "elite" has to be introduced to account for the later presence of the language.

Here we stumble upon the anomalous position of the fortified circular towers known as brochs. These are most abundant in the Atlantic zone: on the Orkney & Shetland islands, Caithness and Sutherland, but with a further prominent (and possibly the oldest) group on Skye; outliers down the west coast as far as Galloway; and another scattered group in the south east along the River Tay, Fife, Stirling and the Borders. They are conspicuously absent from the north-east. Although many are now ruined down to their foundations, a typical broch consisted of double inward-leaning circular dry stone walls, enclosing an area of some 10-12 metres diameter; and with a single fortified entrance. Again, discussion of the broch culture is found within most books about the Celts — but where is the firm evidence for this connection?

In the opinion of Watson, in his 1926 study *The Celtic Place Names of Scotland,* the distribution of the brochs or "Pictish towers" gave support to the legend that the Picts settled first in Orkney and from there raided the northern part of Britain. Watson did not have the benefit of radiocarbon dates. Strictly, the brochs would now have to be associated with the "proto-Picts" rather than the historical Picts, due to the artificial divide that the archaeologists have imposed. Radiocarbon dates for the occupation of the brochs typically fall in a band between the first century BC and the first century AD; often complicated by the fact that many are built on sites of earlier occupation going back as early as 600 BC. They clearly predate the Roman period. Ritchie [*Brochs of Scotland (1988)*] likened them to the later Norman keeps; castles of a conquering aristocracy, designed to overawe an aboriginal subject population.

Perhaps even more interesting though, is the outlying southern group of brochs, such as those at Drumcarrow, Fife and Edinshall, Berwickshire. Those in the Forth valley at Leckie, Stirlingshire and Torwood near Falkirk are the only brochs to show evidence of being taken by force. Indeed Torwood seems to have been built after the Agricolan campaigns and demolished again at some time before or during the Severan campaigns. We therefore have to view these towers as being in some way associated with the Maeatae and their hostile allies against Rome. The occurrence of brochs in the area associated with the Maeatae is a strong argument that they were ethnically linked with the Orcadians.

The following hypothesis is therefore offered. The Maeatae were earlier called Venicontes, which is a Finnic name implying "a boat-tribe". They were Baltic Finnic invaders, probably arriving indirectly as raiders from Orkney. They seized Fife as an easily defensible peninsula and fortified it with brochs at their land borders. This is consistent with the Irish accounts, which say that the Cruithni occupied Britain "from the region of Cat [*Caithness*] to Forchu [*the Forth? Forfar?*]".

When the Romans arrived, the Maeatae and their northern brethren in Orkney and Caithness allied themselves with Rome against the Caledonians and other aboriginal tribes, probably viewing the Romans as a distant and much less immediate threat. This would explain why Agricola did not need to fortify Fife and built his line of forts along Strathmore to protect his allies behind them. The contradictory classical evidence that the Orkney islands submitted to the Claudian Invasion has been given recent support by the discovery of fragments from a Roman amphora at an Orkney broch [*Fitzpatrick (1989)*].

Pausanias makes a curious reference to the confiscation of territory from the Brigantes tribe by the emperor Antoninus. Brigantian territory extended both north and south of Hadrian's wall. They were apparently being punished for invading the territory of a tribe named the *Genuini* who were allied to Rome. Pausanias was contemporary with the events he describes and the unrest must therefore have occurred at some time during the early part of Antoninus' reign (AD 138-161) while the northern wall was under construction. The Genuini may therefore have been a northern tribe; and I have suggested elsewhere that they were the Venicones: the later *Gwyngwn* of the Gododdin. If Pausanias had given us the name of a known tribe, or even no name at all, then we should have no problem in accepting his account as history.

The Romans rapidly withdrew from their northern conquests leaving their client kingdoms nominally subject to the Empire. As tributary allies during the early second century the Maeatae were freely able to settle within the borders of the other British client kingdoms: the Votadini and the Damnonii. They built their brochs there as they had elsewhere and no doubt this caused great resentment among the Britons, leading to local unrest.

It is more likely however, that the seeds of the great revolt during the Severan period ultimately lay in the building of the Antonine Wall. Whatever its strategic merits as viewed from Rome, it divided the territory of the tribal kingdoms without regard to their ethnic differences and prevented free movement of the Maeatae within and beyond the empire's borders. Ultimately some event must have pushed them over the edge into revolt; but unfortunately we may only guess at the priorities of Roman policy during the second century.

In 197, according to Dio, the northern tribes broke some earlier treaty and began raiding the frontier. Following the Severan campaign (AD 208-11) the Maeatae were forced to abandon a part of their territory. They seem to have agreed to this, only to rise again in revolt as soon as the emperor had left.

The Antonine wall could not be defended against a maritime enemy based in Fife, who could simply bypass it. Without the Maeatae as their allies, the Romans could not hold down the Caledonii and Attacotti; they were forced to completely abandon the northern wall and retreat to the frontier of Hadrian. This too may have seemed an adequate frontier while it was protected by a buffer of allies against divided tribes to the north, but once the Caledonii and Maeatae had become a unified enemy, it too was often inadequate to the task.

This revised view of northern ethnography makes far more sense of events on the northern frontier than is gained by viewing all the northern tribes as Celts.

Appendix D

The Pre-historical Pictish King Lists

The Pictish king lists are found in a number of manuscript versions and they differ markedly in the forms of the names and the reigns of the various kings. A comprehensive text and translation of the various lists is available in Skene's *Chronicles*; and they all have been investigated again more recently by M O Anderson, H M Chadwick and others. In a recent study, W A Cummins has correlated the oldest form of the list as given in the *Pictish Chronicle* with the dates in The Annals of Tigernach; and has demonstrated a remarkable degree of correspondence for the historical Pictish period after 565. He, like many other researchers, neglected the pre-historical part of the list. Perhaps we may postulate a comparable degree of reliability for these earlier reigns?

The list overleaf is drawn from Skene's text of the Pictish Chronicle, the pre-historical part is summarised here, solely to give a sense of the chronology of the proto-Pictish period. The approximate dating shown has been obtained by counting back the regnal years from the reign of Brude mac Maelcon.

Name	Reign	Approximate Dating & other comments
Cruithne (and his seven sons)	100 ?	
The Thirty Brudes	150	*[commenced 633 BC]*
Gilgidi [or Gud]	150	
Tharain	100	*[commenced 333 BC]*
Morleo	15	
Deocilmion	40	
Cimoiod son of Arcois	7	
Deoord	50	
Bliesblituth	5	
Dectotr'ic brother of Diu	40	
Usconbuts	30	
Carvorst	40	
Deo ardivois	20	
Uist	50	
Ru	100	*[commenced AD 64]*
Gartnaith	4	
Gartnart	9	
Breth son of Buthut	7	
Uipoig namet	30	
Canutulachama	4	
Wradech uecla	2	
Gartnaich duiberr	60	
Talore son of Achivir	75	
Drust son of Erp	100	"reigned a hundred years and fought a hundred battles. In the nineteenth year of his reign the holy bishop Patrick came to Ireland" *[AD 355-455 corrected to 413-454]*
Talore son of Aniel	4	
Nectan morbet son of Erip	24	"In the third year of his reign, Darlugdach, abbess of Kildare came from Ireland to Britain, in exile for Christ. In the second year of her arrival Nectonius offered up Abernethy [*Apurnethige*] to God and to St Bridget, in the presence of Dairlugdach, who sang Alleluia over this offering..."

Name	Reign	Approximate Dating & other comments
Drest Gurthinmoch	30	
Galanan erilich	12	
Two Drests reigned together	5	
Drest son of Girom (alone)	5	
Garthnac son of Girom	7	
Cailtram son of Girom	1	
Talorg son of Muircholaic	11	
Drest son of Munait	1	
Galam cennaleph	1	
with Bridei	1	
Bridei [*Brude*] son of Maelcon	30	"in the eighth year of his reign he was baptised by Columba" [AD *564 or 565*]

[*There follows the list of kings into the historical Pictish period.*]

The reign of Bridei, or Brude, is the first to be historically verified by other sources and is established at c 556-586 AD, although the Irish annals vary between 554 and 568 for his accession. Other dates shown here are simply achieved by counting back the reigns. The accepted dates for St Patrick suggest that he was born c 395 and was in Ireland at about 432; 19 years before this gives 413 as the approximate date for the commencement of the long reign of Drust. We can only regard his 100 years as indicative of a very long reign. Drust, as king of the Picts is also mentioned in the Annals of Clonmacnoise and Morris's comparison of these with the other Irish annals would indicate that his reign ended somewhere between 453 and 459.

The chronicle shows the period from the accession of Drust to that of Brude mac Maelcon as 202 years, whereas only 143 years are required for the synchronism with St Patrick to be valid. So the reigns have too many years. The loose dates for the beginning and end of Drust's reign enable us to reduce his 100 years to a more credible reign of around 40-46 years. This correlates quite well. If all the subsequent reigns up to Brude mac Maelcon are assumed to be correct then Drust's reign would reduce to 41 years; from 413 to 454.

By a naive count-back of the unadjusted reigns we would arrive at a date early in the first millennium BC for the supposed immigration of the Picts. [*See M O Andersen 1973 p221 for a discussion of the various summae annorum*].

This exercise is plainly of little value as it shows a king Ru, or such like name, supposedly ruling a unified Pictish kingdom at the era when we know that Agricola encountered only a number of divided Caledonian tribes. It is the era of the "thirty Brudes" that comes closest to the true situation described by Tacitus. For much of the following three hundred years, according to other Roman writers, we should expect to find kings of both Caledonii and Maeatae reigning in parallel.

The chronicle shows 838 years between the divided period of the Thirty Brudes and the accession of Drust, whereas from Agricola's conquest (AD 84) to the accession of Drust (est 413) would occupy only 329 years. This may indicate that the early reigns are all the invention of some dark-age chronicler, who was completely unaware of the Roman sources. The Brudes, however, have a ring of truth about them; for why would anyone wish to invent such an enigmatic list? If the earliest kings are real, then possibly king lists of Maeatae and Caledonii have been merged at some point. Some of the strangest names may even be kings from other contemporary tribal groups. The merger of separate lists of kings reigning in parallel might explain the long chronology that we see. After all, an analogous situation is observed in Manetho's list of the ancient Egyptian kings.

Another way to analyse the early part of the king list might be to average the reign lengths. The longer reigns, with rounded numbers of years, have to be immediately suspected. The average reign length for the 13 kings from Drust to the accession of Brude mac Maelcon is just over 15.5 years (unadjusted) or 12 years if Drust's reign is adjusted as above. If we substitute this average reign for the 21 reigns from Gilgidi to the accession of Drust, we may obtain an estimated date for the accession of Gilgidi and the close of the era of the Thirty Brudes; this would give AD 87 (unadjusted) or AD 161 (adjusted).

Either estimate would then allow the Thirty Brudes to become contemporary with Agricola; one of whom: Brude Cal/Ur-Cal may therefore be that *Calgacus* named by Tacitus as only one among many chiefs. Similarly, the era of the Pictish immigration could then be brought forward to a more credible date of about 100 BC.

Appendix E

Previous Interpretations of the Pictish Names and Places

The following table shows a representative sample of the various Celtic interpretations of Pictish place and tribal names that have been proposed to date. Each will lead the researcher to earlier references. They are respectively: MacBain (1891), Jackson (1955) and Rivett & Smith (1979). At the right is given a suggested alternative Finnic derivation, where applicable.

Abbreviations:
B = British, G = Gaelic, Ga = Gaulish, C = Celtic, L = Latin, Gr = Greek, I E = Indo-European

Word	Source	MacBain	Jackson	Rivett/Smith	Finnic?
Caledonii	various	B. celli "woodlanders"	not Celtic	C. *calet- "hard", "tough"	kalaton "no-fish"
Venicones Venicontes	Ptolemy	B.. gwern-cwn "marsh dogs"	not Celtic	C. *ueni "kindred race"	venekunta "a boat's crew"
Taexali	Ptolemy		not Celtic	derivation	taistelija
Taezali	Ptolemy			obscure	"fighters"
Vacomagi	Ptolemy	B. gwag + G. magh "empty-plains"	not Celtic *mago	I.E. *uek + "strong-men" "empty- fields"	väki+miehet
Lugi Logi	Ptolemy	Luga (a Gaulish god)	P-Celtic	Ga.. Lougos "black", "dark"	lohi "salmon"
Smertae Mertae	Ptolemy	Ga.. smer- "shine"	Gallo-Brittonic	C. *smer- "smeared folk"	not Finnic
Cornovii Carnabi	Ptolemy	C. corn-	Gallo-	B. Corn- "horn-folk"	
Caerini	Ptolemy	Ga.. caora "sheep"		B. caoro- "sheep"	karinen "rocks" "reefs"

Word	Source	MacBain	Jackson	Rivett/Smith	Finnic?
Carnonace	Ptolemy	C. carn- "hill-people"	P-Celtic	C. carn- "hill-people"	
Creones Cerones	Ptolemy	C. kre- "cut", "throw"		C. Cre- unknown meaning	not Finnic
Decantae Cantae	Ptolemy	L. Decus "glory"	P-Celtic	C. *Dec- "good", "noble"	
Epidii	Ptolemy	Ga. Epo- "horse"	Gallo-Brittonic	B. *epos "horse"	
Damnonii Dumnonii	Ptolemy	Ga. Domhan "deep"		B. "worshippers of Dumnonos"	
Votadini	Ptolemy			descendants of Fothad	
Novantae	Ptolemy			C. novio "new tribe"	
Maeatae	Dio Cassius			C. maia "people of the larger part"	miehet "the men"

Word	Source	MacBain	Jackson	Rivett/Smith	Finnic?
Verturiones	Ammianus			C. *uer + *treno "very strong ones"	voitta- "victorious ones"
Attecotti	Ammianus			C. *ate- + *cotto "very-old ones"	not Finnic
Boresti	Tacitus			unknown	not Finnic
Niduari	Bede				noita "Druids" "magicians"
Peanfahel	Bede		Penn + Fáil "end of wall"		pyhiinvaellus "holy wandering" "pilgrimage"
Orcas Orcades	Pytheas	I.E. or "ran", "start"	G. Orci young pigs	G. *Orcoi + Gr as/ades	
Nabarus (Naver)	Ptolemy	G. navis "ship"		I.E. *nabh + ar "cloud-water"	neva "peat bog"

Word	Source	MacBain	Jackson	Rivett/Smith	Finnic?
Varrar (Farrar)	Ptolemy	L. var- "winding" "bending"		I.E. root "water"	väärä "crooked"
Loxa (Lossie)	Ptolemy	B. lok-s "oblique" "shining"	Gr loxos "crooked"	C. losc "winding"	lossi "ferry"
Caelis	Ptolemy	G. Caol "narrow"		unknown	kahla "ford"
Tuesis	Ptolemy	B. chwgd "vomit"	not Celtic	unknown	tuhis "hissing" "noisy"
Graupius	Tacitus		not Q-Celtic	unknown	not Finnic

Bibliography

Bibliographies of Pictish and other Sources

A comprehensive bibliography of studies relating to the Picts is that of Dr J R F Burt in Nicol, E (ed) *A Pictish Panorama* (Pinkfoot Press, Balgavies, Angus, 1995) - which includes known works in preparation at that date. Earlier bibliographies may also be found in:

Friell, J G P and Watson, W G (eds), *Pictish Studies: settlement, burial and art in Dark Age northern Britain* (Oxford, 1984)
Wainwright, F T (ed) *The Problem of the Picts* (Perth, 1955 [repr 1980])

A select bibliography of works relating to Roman Britain and the northern frontier is available in:

Ireland, S, *Roman Britain - A Sourcebook* (London, Second Edition, 1996)
Salway, P, *Roman Britain* (Oxford, 1981)

A starting point for the Dark-Age sources, including Welsh and Irish Annals is:

Morris, J (ed), *Arthurian Period Sources*, Volume 1 (Phillimore, Chichester, 1995)

Translations and Editions

For many of the historical sources relevant to Pictish origins, no complete translation or critical edition in English is as yet available, whereas others may be difficult to obtain. Selected and translated extracts relating to Britain may be found in:

Petrie, H, *Monumenta Historica Britannica* (London, 1848 [reprinted 1969])

Ireland, S, *Roman Britain - A Sourcebook* (London, Second Edition, 1996)

Other translations used in this study are:

Anderson, A O, *Early Sources of Scottish History, AD 500-1286*, Volume 1 (Oliver & Boyd, Edinburgh, 1922)

Anderson, W B, *Sidonius*, Vol 1 (Harvard University Press, Cambridge, Massachusets, 1936)

Bromwich, R, *Troiedd Ynys Prydein* (Cardiff, 1961 [repr 1978])

Bromwich, R, Troiedd Ynys Prydain: The Myvyrian "Third Series", in *Transactions of the Honourable Society of Cymmrodorion*, Part 1, 299-335 (1968)

Bromwich, R, Troiedd Ynys Prydain: The Myvyrian "Third Series", in *Transactions of the Honourable Society of Cymmrodorion*, Part 2, 127-156 (1969)

Cary, E, *Dio Cassius*, Vol 9 (Harvard University Press, Cambridge, Massachusets, 1982)

Cherniss, H and Hembold, W C, *Plutarch: Moralia*, Vol 12 (Harvard University Press, Cambridge, Massachusets, 1957)

Colgrave, B, *Two Lives of St Cuthbert* (Cambridge, 1940)

De Selincourt, A *Herodotus: The Histories* (Penguin, Harmondsworth, 1954 [repr 1988])

Duff, J D, *Lucan-The Civil War (Pharsalia)* (Harvard University Press, Cambridge, Massachusets, 1928)

Echols, E C H, *Herodian of Antioch* (Univ of California, 1961)

Forbes, A P (ed), *Lives of St Ninian and St Kentigern* (Historians of Scotland, Edinburgh 1874)

Golding A, *Solinus - Collectanea Rerum Memorabilium* (1587, reprinted in facsimile by Scholars Facsimiles and reprints, Gainsville, Florida, 1955)

Handford, S A, *Caesar-The Conquest of Gaul* (Penguin, Harmondsworth, 1951)

Hood, A B, *Saint Patrick - His Writings and Muirchu's Life* (Phillimore, London, 1978)

Jones, H L, *The Geography of Strabo* (Harvard University Press, Cambridge, Massachusets, 1988)

MacBain, A, "Ptolemy's Geography of Scotland" in *Transactions of the Gaelic Society of Inverness*, 21 (1891-92), 191-214 (1892)

Mattingley, H, *Tacitus - the Agricola and the Germania* (Penguin, Harmondsworth, 1989)

Morris, J, *Nennius, British History and the Welsh Annals* (Phillimore, London, 1980)

Murphy, Rev D (ed), *The Annals of Clonmacnoise* (Univ of Dublin, 1896)

Oldfather, C H, *Diodorus Siculus*, Vol 3 (Harvard University Press, Cambridge, Massachusets, 1993)

Pennar, M, *Taliesin Poems* (Llanerch, Felinfach 1988)

Platnauer, M, *Claudian* (Harvard University Press, Cambridge, Massachusets, 1922)

Potter, T W, *Roman Britain* (British Museum Press, London 1997)

Rackham, H, *Pliny - Natural History*, Vol 2 (Harvard University Press, Cambridge, Massachusets, 1989)

Reeves, W, *Adamnan - Life of Saint Columba* (Historians of Scotland, Edmonston 1874)

Robinson, S, *Juvenal - Sixteen Satires upon the Ancient Harlot* (Carcanet New Press, Manchester, 1983)

Rolfe, J C, *Ammianus Marcellinus*, vol III (Harvard University Press, Cambridge, Massachusets, 1939)

Shackleton-Bailey, D R, *Martial-Epigrams* (Harvard University Press, Cambridge, Massachusets, 1993)

Sherley-Price, L, *Bede- A History of the English Church and People* (Penguin, Harmondsworth, 1968)

Skene, W F, *Chronicles of the Picts, Chronicles of the Scots, and other early Memorials of Scottish History* (Edinburgh, 1867)

Skene, W F, *Four Ancient Books of Wales* (Edinburgh, 1868)

Skene, W F, *John of Fordun's Chronicle of the Scottish Nation* (Edinburgh 1872)

Stokes, W, *The Annals of Tigernach* ([reprinted from *Revue Celtique* 1895/96] Llanerch, Felinfach 1993)

Thorpe, L, *Geoffrey of Monmouth: The History of the Kings of Britain* (Penguin, Harmondsworth, 1966 [repr 1987])

Watt, D E R (ed), *Scotichronicon by Walter Bower, in Latin and English*, volume 1 (Mercat Press, Edinburgh, 1993)

Winterbottom, M, *Gildas - The Ruin of Britain and other Documents* (Phillimore, London, 1978)

Texts

Where a translation is available, this will usually refer to the source text from which it was taken. Latin and Greek texts for selected fragments relating to Britain are available in the *Monumenta Historica Britannica*. Other source texts used here are:

Anderson, J G C, *Tacitus: Germania*, Clarendon (Oxford, 1938)

Caerwyn-Williams, J E, *The Poems of Taliesin* (Dublin, 1987)

Galletier, E, *Panegyrici Latini* (Paris, 1949)

Jones, O (ed), *The Myvyrian Archaiology of Wales* (Denbigh, 1870)

Lindsay, W M, *Isidori Hispalensis Episcopi Etymologiarum sive Origines*, V1 & II (Clarendon, Oxford, 1911)

Meyer, K, *Sanas Cormaic* (Dublin 1913 [reprinted, Llanerch, Felinfach, 1994])

Migne, J P, *Patrologia Latina*, (vols XXII & XXII) (1844)

Mommsen, T, *C Iulii Solini* (Berlin 1895 [reprinted 1958])

Parroni, P, *Pomponii Melae* (De Chorographia, Rome, 1984)

Pictish Studies (with an emphasis on language and ethnic origins):

Allen, J R and Anderson, J, *The Early Christian Monuments of Scotland*, Society of Antiquaries of Scotland (Edinburgh, 1903)

Anderson, A O, Scottish Annals from English Chroniclers AD 500-1286 (David Nutt, London, 1908)

Anderson, M O, "The Scottish Materials in the Paris Manuscript", Bib Nat Latin 4126, *Scottish Historical Review*, 28 (1950), 13-22

Anderson, M O, (revised 1980)*Kings and Kingship in Early Scotland*, Scottish Academic Press (Edinburgh, 1973)

Anderson, M O, "Picts: the Name and the People", in Small, A (ed), *The Picts - A New Look at Old Problems* (Dundee, 1987), 7-14

Childe, V G, *Scotland before the Scots* (London, 1946)

Chadwick, H M, *Early Scotland: the Picts, the Scots and the Welsh of Southern Scotland*, (Cambridge University Press, Cambridge, 1949)

Chadwick, N K, "The Name Pict", *Scottish Gaelic Studies*, 8, 146-76 (1958)

Clarkson, T J, "The Gododdin and the Picts", *Pictish Arts Society Journal* (Autumn 1992), 2-4

Clement, R D, "The Languages of the Picts", in Burt, J R F et al, *Stones, Symbols and Stories, Aspects of Pictish Studies* (Edinburgh, 1994), 3-4

Cummins, W A, *The Age of the Picts* (Alan Sutton Publishing, Stroud, 1995)

Diack, F C, *The Inscriptions of Pictland* (Spalding Club, Aberdeen, 1944)

Forsyth, K, "Language in Pictland, spoken and written" in Nicol, E (ed) *A Pictish Panorama* (Balgavies, Angus 1995)

Foster, S M, *Picts, Gaels and Scots* (B T Batsford, Ltd, London 1996)

Fraser, I A, "Pictish Place Names: Some Toponymic Evidence" in Small, A (ed), *The Picts - A New Look at Old Problems* (Dundee, 1987), 68-72

Fraser, J, *History and Etymology* (Clarendon Press, Oxford, 1923)

Friell, J G P and Watson, W G, *Pictish Studies: Settlement, Burial and Art in Dark Age Northern Britain*, British Archaeological Reports 125 (Oxford ,1984)

Graham-Campbell, J, "A lost Pictish treasure (and two Viking-age gold arm-rings) from the Broch of Burgar, Orkney", *Proc Soc Antiq Scot*, 115 (1985), 241-261

Guiter, H "La Langue des Pictes", *Boletin de la Real Sociedad Vascoganda de los Amigos del Pais (San Sebastian)*, 24:281-321 (1968)

Henderson, I, *The Picts* (Thames and Hudson, London 1967)

Henderson, I, "The Picts: Written records and Pictorial Images" in Burt, J R F et al, *Stones, Symbols and Stories Aspects of Pictish Studies* (Edinburgh, 1994) 44-66

Hubert, H, *The Rise of the Celts* (London, 1934)

Hudson, B T "Historical Literature of Early Scotland", *Studies in Scottish Literature*, 26, 141-55 (1991)

Innes, T, "A critical essay on the ancient inhabitants of the northern parts of Britain or Scotland, *Historians of Scotland, VIII* (Edinburgh 1729, [repr 1885])

Jackson, A, *The Symbol Stones of Scotland* (The Orkney Press, Stromness, 1984)

Jackson, K H, "The Pictish Language" in Wainwright, F T (ed), *The Problem of the Picts* (Edinburgh, 1955) 129-60

Jackson, K H, *The Gododdin: The Oldest Scottish Poem* (Edinburgh Univ Press, Edinburgh, 1969)

Jackson, K H, *The Gaelic Notes in the Book of Deer* (Cambridge University Press, Cambridge, 1972)

Johnstone, J B, *The Place Names of Scotland* (S R Publishers, Edinburgh, 1892)

Johnstone, P, *The Sea Craft of Prehistory* (Routledge, London, 1980)

Koch, J T, "The Stone of the Wenicones", *Bulletin of the Board of Celtic Studies*, 29, 87-89 (1980)

Koch, J T, "The Loss of Final Syllables and Loss of Declension in Brittonic", *Bulletin of the Board of Celtic Studies*, 30, 201-33 (1983)

Lethbridge, T C, *The Painted Men* (London, 1954)

Levinson, W, *An Eighth-century Poem on St Ninian*, Antiquity, XIV (1940) 280-291

McHardy, S, "The Folklore of the Picts" in Burt, J R F, et al (eds) *Stones, Symbols and Stories Aspects of Pictish Studies* (Edinburgh, 1994) 33-38

Macalister, R A S "The Inscriptions and Language of the Northern Picts", in Ryan, J (ed), *Essays and Studies presented to Professor Eoin MacNeill* (Dublin 1940), 184-226

MacBain, A, "Ptolemy's Geography of Scotland", *Transactions of the Gaelic Society of Inverness*, 21 (1896-97), 191-214 (1892)

MacNeill, E, "The Pretanic Background in Britain and Ireland", *J Roy Soc Antiq Ir*, 63, 1-28 (1933)

MacNeill, E, "The Language of the Picts", *Yorkshire Celtic Studies*, 2, (1938-39), 3-45

Mahr, A, "New Aspects and Problems in Irish Prehistory", *Proceedings of the Prehistoric Society*, III (1937), 262-436

Miller, M, "Stilicho's Pictish War", *Britannia*, 6 (1975), 141-45

Miller, M, "The Disputed Historical Horizon of the Pictish King Lists", *Scottish Historical Review*, 58 (1979), 1-34

Nicolaisen, W H F, *Scottish Place Names: their study and significance* (Batsford, London 1976)

Nicolaisen, W H F, "Pictish Place Names", in Nicol, E (ed), *A Pictish Panorama* (Balgavies, Angus, 1995)

O' Rahilly, T F, *Early Irish History and Mythology* (Dublin Institute for Advanced Studies, Dublin, 1946)

Pinkerton, J, *An Enquiry into the History of Scotland preceding the Reign of Malcolm III* (Edinburgh, 1789)

Pokorny, J, *Zur Urgeschichte der Kelten and Illyrier* (Halle, 1938)

Ralston, I And Inglis, J, *Foul Hordes: the Picts in the North-East and their Background* (Aberdeen, 1984)

Reeves, W, *The Culdees of the British Islands, as They Appear in History: with an Appendix of Evidences* (Dublin, 1864 [reprinted Llanerch, Felinfach, 1994])

Rivet, A L F and Smith, C, *The Place Names of Roman Britain* (Batsford, London, 1979)

Rhys, J, *The Rhind Lectures in Archaeology: The Early Ethnology of the British Isles*, (1890-91, reprinted Llanerch, Felinfach, 1990)

Rhys, J, "The Inscriptions and Language of the Northern Picts", *Proc Soc Antiq Scot*, 26 (1891-92), 263-351 (1892)

Rhys, J, "The Inscriptions and Language of the Northern Picts (Addenda & Corrigenda)", *Proc Soc Antiq Scot*, 27 (1892-93), 411-12 (1893)

Rhys, J, "A revised Account of the Inscriptions of the Northern Picts", *Proc Soc Antiq Scot*, 26 (1897-98), 324-98 (1898)

Skene, W F, *The Highlanders of Scotland* (second edition, 1902) (Stirling, 1836)

Skene, W F, *Celtic Scotland A History of Ancient Alban*, 3 vols (Edinburgh, 1876-80, [revised edition, 1886-1890])

Smyth, A P, *Warlords and Holy Men: Scotland AD 80-1000* (London, 1984)

Sutherland, E, *In Search of the Picts A Celtic Dark Age Nation* (Constable, London, 1994)

Stokes, W, "On the linguistic value of the Irish Annals", *Transactions of the Philological Society*, (1888-90), 365-433 (1890)

Wainright, F T, "The Picts and the Problem" in Wainright, F T (ed) *The Problem of the Picts* (Edinburgh 1955)

Wainwright, F T (ed), *The Northern Isles*, Nelson (Edinburgh, 1962)

Watson, W J, *The History of the Celtic Place-names of Scotland* (Edinburgh and London, 1926)

Whittington, G and Soulsby, J A, A Preliminary Report on an Investigation into PIT Place Names, *Scottish Geographical Magazine*, 84,2,117-125 (1968)

Miscellaneous

Bergland, K Norwegian research on the Language and Folklore of the Lapps Part 1, Language, *Journal of Royal Anthropological Institute*, vol LXXX (1950)

Brothwell, D, *The Bog Man and the Archaeology of People* (London, 1976)

Bryce, D, (ed) *Arthur and the Britons in Wales and Scotland: by W F Skene* (Llanerch Felinfach, 1988)

Bolton, J D P, *Aristeas of Proconnesus* (Oxford, 1962)

Christiansen, R T, Norwegian Research on the Language and Folklore of the Lapps, part 2, Mythology and Folklore, *Journal of Royal Anthropological Institute*, vol LXXX (1950)

Clarke, B, Calidon and the Caledonian Forest, *Bulletin of the Board of Celtic Studies*, 23,191-201 (1969)

Darton, M, *The Dictionary of Scottish Place Names* (Lochar Publishing, Moffat 1990)

Fitzpatrick, A P, "The Submission of the Orkney Islands to Claudius: New evidence", *Scottish Archaeological Review*, 6:24-33 (1989)

Hajdu, P, *Finno-Ugrian Languages and Peoples,* translated by G Cushing (Andre Deutch, London, 1974)

Hakulinen, L, *The Structure and Development of the Finnish Language* (translated by J Atkinson) (Indianna Univ Press, Bloomington, Indianna 1961)

Hind, J G F, "The British 'Provinces' of Valentia and Orcades", *Historia* 24, 101-11 (1975)

Hind, J G F, "The 'Genounian' part of Britain", *Britannia* 8, 229-34 (1977)

Holmberg, U, "Finno-Ugric Mythology" in *Mythology of All Races*, volume 4 (Boston, 1964)

Keppie, L, *Scotland's Roman Remains*, John Donald (Edinburgh, 1986)

Koppana, K M, *The Finnish Gods*, Mandragora (Helsinki, 1990)

Koppana, K M, *Snakefat and Knotted Threads: A Short Introduction to Traditional Finnish Magic* (Mandragora, Helsinki, 1990)

Koppana, K M, *Forest Spirits*, (Mandragora, Helsinki, 1992)

Lockwood, W B, *The Languages of the British Isles* (Andre Deutch, London, 1975)

Macinnes, L, "Brochs and the Roman occupation of Lowland Scotland", *Proc Soc Antiq Scot*, 114 (1984), 235-49 (1984)

Mackie, E W, "English Migrants and Scottish Brochs", *Glasgow Archaeological Journal*, 2:39-71 (1971)

Mackie, E W, "The Leckie broch, Stirlingshire, an interim report", *Glasgow Archaeological Journal*, 9: 59-72 (1982)

Mackie, E W and Rona, M, "Red-haired 'Celts' are better termed Caledonians", *American Journal of Dermatopathology*, 6 (Supplement 1), 147-9 (1984)

Mackie, E W, "Leckie broch: impact on the Scottish Iron Age", *Glasgow Archaeological Journal*, 14:1-18 (1987)

Mackie, E W, "The Early Celts in Scotland", in Green, M J (ed) *The Celtic World* (Routledge, London, 1995)

Mayor, A and Heaney, M, "Griffins and Arimaspians", *Folklore*, 104, 40-66 (1993)

Morris, J, *The Age of Arthur A History of the British Isles from 350 to 650* (Weidenfeld and Nicolson, London 1973)

Morris, J (ed) *Arthurian Sources, volume 2, Annals and Charters* (Phillimore, Chichester, 1995)

Morris, J (ed), *Arthurian Sources, volume 4, Places and Peoples and Saxon Archaeology* (Phillimore, Chichester, 1995)

Morris, J (ed) *Arthurian Sources, volume 6, Studies in Dark Age History* (Phillimore, Chichester, 1995)

Muhlberger, S, "The Gallic Chronicle of 452 and its Authority for British Events", *Britannia*, 14 pp 23-33 (1983)

Peabody-Magoun Jr, F (tr), *The Old Kalevala - Elias Lohnrot* (Harvard, 1969)

Price, G, *The Languages of Britain* (Edward Arnold, London, 1984)

Renfrew, C, *Archaeology and Language: The Puzzle of Indo-European Origins* (Johnathan Cape, London, 1987)

Rice-Holmes, T, *Ancient Britain and the Invasions of Julius Caesar* (Oxford University Press, 1936)

Ritchie, J N G, *Brochs of Scotland* (Shire, Aylesbury, 1988)

Rolle, R, *The World of the Scythians* (Berkley, California, 1989)

Rudenko, S I, *The Frozen Tombs of Siberia* (London, 1970)

Vorren, O and Manker, E, *Lapp Life and Customs: a Survey* (OUP 1962)

Wright, R P, "Carpow and Caracalla", *Britannia* 5, 289-92 (1974)

Index

Caesar, Julius 16, 22, 34, 50, 63, 68, 93
Cait, 6, 45, 81, 82
Caithness, 6, 26, 28, 62, 85, 87, 88, 106, 107
Caledonia, 3, 19, 24, 26, 30, 53, 57, 59, 67, 105
Caledonii, 9, 10, 12, 19, 21, 23, 24, 25, 30, 33, 34, 43, 44, 45, 56, 58, 108, 112, 114
Calgacus, 9, 25, 30, 53, 112
Camber, 6
cannibalism, 67, 96, 101 (see also Androphagi)
Caracalla, 12
Carpow, 12
Ce, 6, 45, 81, 82
Celtic Church, 14, 35, 37
Celtic languages,vii, 3, 6, 7, 15, 16, 17, 19, 22, 25, 27, 28, 29, 30, 42, 43, 44, 100, 105, 106, 113, 114, 115, 117
Celts, 3, 15, 17, 29, 30, 37, 43, 44, 45, 94, 96, 97, 100, 105, 106, 108
Chadwick, 66, 109
Christianity, 1, 13, 14, 29, 34, 35, 37 39, 41, 44
Chronicle of 452, 69
Claudian, 13, 63, 65, 66-67
Claudian Invasion, 8, 65, 107
Claudius, 10, 51, 78, 87
Clonmacnoise, Annals of, 3, 69, 89-90 111
Colchester, 25, 61
Collessie Man, 36
Constantine, 64
Constantius, 12, 63, 64, 69
Cormac, 74, 79, 80
Cornovii, 25, 44, 114
Cruithne, 6, 33, 34, 81, 110
Cruithni, 3, 5, 12, 25, 41, 44, 80, 83, 84, 96, 97, 104, 107
Cruthin, 3, 25
Cruthneach, 3, 6, 33, 80, 81, 82, 83
Culdees, 40
Cuthbert, Saint, 14, 42, 74, 75, 85

Dalriada, 2, 14, 27
De Situ Albanie, 6, 85
Dealreudians, 2, 76
demons, 40, 41
Diack, F C, 16, 35, 53, 61
Dicalydones, 12, 24, 65
Dio Cassius, 10, 20, 22, 25, 33, 34, 36, 45, 50, 58-60, 68, 76, 93, 115
Diodorus Siculus, 8, 27, 50, 96-97
Dneiper, 95, 98, 99
Druids, 41, 73
Drust, 33, 89, 110, 111, 112
Edward I, 5
Epidii, 25, 44, 56, 115
Essedones, 30, 98, 100
Estonians, 15, 23, 24, 27, 30, 42, 44, 103
Eusebius, 64
Eutropius, 51, 65, 67, 76
Fenni, 100, 101, 104
Fife, 6, 9, 10, 12, 22, 23, 36, 58, 61, 85, 106, 107, 108
Finnic languages, 15, 16, 21, 22, 23, 26, 27, 28, 31, 42, 43, 44, 103-104
fish, 20, 21, 58, 114
Fordun, John of, 4
Fraser, J, 16
Gaelic, 1, 3, 4, 7, 14, 15, 16, 27, 28, 29, 38, 44, 113
Galloway, 42, 69, 75, 85, 86, 106
Gaul, 5, 10, 12, 22, 52, 67, 83
Geloni, 93, 95, 98, 104
Genuini, 55, 107
Geoffrey of Monmouth, 6, 87-88
geographers (classical), 3, 4, 8
Germania, 30, 99
Germanus, Saint, 69, 89
Gildas, 13, 22, 33, 70-71, 93
goddesses, 39, 41, 100
Gododdin, 22, 40, 55, 72, 107
Golding Arthur, 61, 101
Gothic, 16, 66, 104
Goths, 16, 30, 79
Grampian Mountains, 9
Graupius, 9, 25, 30, 53, 104, 117